The Abyss

Psychoanalytic Inquiry Book Series

Volume 37

PSYCHOANALYTIC INQUIRY BOOK SERIES

JOSEPH D. LICHTENBERG
Series Editor

Like its counterpart, *Psychoanalytic Inquiry: A Topical Journal for Mental Health Professionals*, the Psychoanalytic Inquiry Book Series presents a diversity of subjects within a diversity of approaches to those subjects. Under the editorship of Joseph Lichtenberg, in collaboration with Melvin Bornstein and the editorial board of *Psychoanalytic Inquiry*, the volumes in this series strike a balance between research, theory, and clinical application. We are honored to have published the works of various innovators in psychoanalysis, such as Frank Lachmann, James Fosshage, Robert Stolorow, Donna Orange, Louis Sander, Léon Wurmser, James Grotstein, Joseph Jones, Doris Brothers, Fredric Busch, and Joseph Lichtenberg, among others.

The series includes books and monographs on mainline psychoanalytic topics, such as sexuality, narcissism, trauma, homosexuality, jealousy, envy, and varied aspects of analytic process and technique. In our efforts to broaden the field of analytic interest, the series has incorporated and embraced innovative discoveries in infant research, self psychology, intersubjectivity, motivational systems, affects as process, responses to cancer, borderline states, contextualism, postmodernism, attachment research and theory, medication, and mentalization. As further investigations in psychoanalysis come to fruition, we seek to present them in readable, easily comprehensible writing.

After 25 years, the core vision of this series remains the investigation, analysis, and discussion of developments on the cutting edge of the psychoanalytic field, inspired by a boundless spirit of inquiry.

PSYCHOANALYTIC INQUIRY BOOK SERIES

JOSEPH D. LICHTENBERG
Series Editor

The Abyss
of Madness

George E. Atwood

Routledge
Taylor & Francis Group
New York   London

Routledge
Taylor & Francis Group
711 Third Avenue
New York, NY 10017

Routledge
Taylor & Francis Group
27 Church Road
Hove, East Sussex BN3 2FA

© 2012 by Taylor & Francis Group, LLC
Routledge is an imprint of Taylor & Francis Group, an Informa business

Printed in the United States of America on acid-free paper
Version Date: 20110525

International Standard Book Number: 978-0-415-89709-9 (Hardback) 978-0-415-89710-5 (Paperback)

Library of Congress Cataloging-in-Publication Data

Atwood, George E.
    The abyss of madness : clinical explorations / George E. Atwood.
        p. cm. -- (Psychoanalytic inquiry book series ; v. 37)
    Includes bibliographical references and index.
    ISBN 978-0-415-89709-9 (hardback) -- ISBN 978-0-415-89710-5 (paperback)
    -- ISBN 978-0-203-69783-2 (e-book)
    1. Psychotherapist and patient--Case studies. 2. Psychoanalysis--Case studies.
3. Mental illness. I. Title.

    RC480.8.A887 2012
    616.89'14--dc23   2011017345

Visit the Taylor & Francis Web site at
http://www.taylorandfrancis.com

and the Routledge Web site at
http://www.routledgementalhealth.com

Contents

Acknowledgments

I wish to thank first of all my wife, Liz Atwood, who has encouraged me to write a book such as this one for many years, and who gave support and love at every stage in its completion. I am indebted as well to my daughter, Rebecca Atwood, who after reading early chapters of the manuscript gave penetrating criticism and wonderful advice that have been incorporated into its final form. And in addition, I want to acknowledge the contribution of my son, Christopher Atwood, who was the first to tell me, with great emphasis, that I should convert some informal essays I had written for my students into a book for a wider audience.

A great many students, colleagues, and friends have also helped me in manifold ways in completing this work, giving generously of their time and energy and offering valuable suggestions. I thank them all from the bottom of my heart.

Some of the chapters in the book are revisions of articles published in various journals:

Chapter 1 appeared in *Pragmatic Case Studies in Psychotherapy* (2011, 7).

Chapters 2 and 3 are revisions of papers that were published in *International Journal of Psychoanalytic Self Psychology* (2010, 5(3), pp. 334–356; 2011, 6(1), pp. 99–112; 2011, 6(2), pp. 1–6; 2011, 6(3), pp. 1–9; 2011, 6(4).

Chapter 4 is a rewritten version of a paper appearing in *Annual of Psychoanalysis* (2010/2011, *37/38*, pp. 205–220).

Chapter 9 is a revision of a paper published originally in *Psychoanalytic Review* (2011, 98(3), pp. 263–285).

I thank the editors of these journals for their permission to reprint the various articles. I am also grateful to the estate of Martin Ramirez for granting permission to use one of this artist's images for which it holds the copyright.

Prologue

In my work as a psychotherapist exploring the far reaches of madness, I have discovered something completely unexpected: myself. Amid the shattered hearts, the broken minds, the annihilations—it is as if the pattern of my own life and world has been somehow inscribed. Does this mean I should be diagnosed, medicated, and, perhaps, taken away? I certainly hope not. Another possibility is that the individuals we consider insane are simply human, all too human, and the pathways their lives have followed are also our own. What if the territory of the so-called psychoses is the mirror of our souls, given to us with extravagant clarity and drama? What if the task of studying and understanding madness is also an opportunity for us to discover who we actually are?

Extreme psychological disturbances often present themselves in obscure, incomprehensible forms. And yet, no matter how difficult the symptoms may be to understand, these conditions remain, in their essential being, human events arising out of human contexts. But it is not just that. When we listen to the human stories told by our most disturbed patients, we inevitably also rediscover ourselves. A central aim of this book is to erase the sharp boundary that has been drawn to separate madness from sanity, returning the phenomena of severe psychological disorders to the circle of the humanly intelligible.

The viewpoint guiding this work is that of *phenomenological contextualism*, a perspective that has gradually come into being over the course of many decades of collaborative study, primarily with Robert Stolorow (Stolorow & Atwood, 1979; Atwood & Stolorow, 1984, 1993), but importantly as well with Bernard Brandchaft (Stolorow, Brandchaft, & Atwood, 1987) and Donna Orange (Orange, Atwood, & Stolorow, 1997; Stolorow, Atwood, & Orange, 2002). Born originally of studies of the subjective origins of psychoanalytic theories, this way of understanding has arisen out of our efforts, over more than three decades, to rethink psychoanalysis as a form of phenomenological inquiry and to illuminate the phenomenology of the psychoanalytic process itself. Our dedication to phenomenological inquiry, in turn, led us to a contextualist theoretical perspective, from which personal worlds of emotional experience are always seen as embedded in constitutive relational contexts.

This evolution has had profound consequences for our understanding of psychoanalytic theory and of the varied phenomena it seeks to address, including our conceptions of psychological structure, of the unconscious, of psychological development, of dreams, of trauma, of the phenomena of psychopathology in all of its variations and degrees of severity, and of the psychotherapeutic process. Phenomenological contextualism is a post-Cartesian viewpoint, dispensing with a view of the person as an isolated mind—a thinking thing having contents that looks out upon a world from which it is essentially estranged. Instead, the legacy of the philosophy of Descartes is replaced by a broadly based set of assumptions on which the person is seen as always inhabiting a world that provides the context for his or her experiences, a world itself understood as saturated by human meanings and purposes.

Traditional Freudian theory and its derivatives are pervaded by the Cartesian myth of the isolated mind (Stolorow & Atwood, 1992), which bifurcates the experiential world into inner and outer regions, severs both mind from body and cognition from affect, reifies and absolutizes the resulting divisions, and pictures the mind as an objective entity that takes its place among other objects. Freud's psychoanalysis greatly expanded the Cartesian mind to include a vast unconscious realm. Nevertheless, the Freudian psyche remained a Cartesian mind, a self-enclosed mental apparatus containing and working over mental contents, a thinking *thing* that, precisely because it is a thing, is decontextualized, fundamentally separated from its world. Phenomenological contextualism, by contrast, leads to a post-Cartesian psychoanalysis that investigates and illuminates emotional experience as it takes form within constitutive relational contexts. From a post-Cartesian perspective, all the phenomena that have traditionally been the focus of psychoanalytic investigation are grasped not as products of isolated intrapsychic mechanisms but as forming within systems constituted by interacting worlds of emotional experience.

The philosophical foundations of phenomenological contextualism trace back to the thinking of a number of post-Cartesian philosophers, most notably Søren Kierkegaard, Friedrich Nietzsche, Ludwig Wittgenstein, and especially Martin Heidegger (Atwood, Stolorow, & Orange, 2011; Stolorow, 2011). My purpose in this book, however, is not to focus on such historical origins, but rather to give a more purely clinical exposition, illustrating the radical implications of this viewpoint for the practice of psychotherapy.

This book presents a series of specific clinical stories and includes detailed accounts of individuals in crisis and of the successes and failures that occurred in their treatment. This material reflects the almost 50 years I have spent working as a psychotherapist, teaching, writing, and thinking about the problem of madness in all of its many aspects. The topics covered range widely, addressing the most extreme emotional situations human beings may fall into. I focus on different forms of psychosis, major depression and suicide, the impact on people of profound childhood trauma, the splintering of personality into systems of alternative selves, the psychotherapy of extreme states, the relation of madness to genius, and the importance of the philosophical premises of clinicians working with severe psychological disturbances. The final chapter approaches the philosophers whose thinking made phenomenological contextualism possible. By viewing these great thinkers as clinical cases, I have tried to point toward a future in which even their ideas are superseded. Throughout the discussions, an emphasis is always placed on discovering the inner truth of a life, and I do not think it is possible to read the accounts without being brought closer to the truths lying at the heart of one's own personal existence.

1

Psychotherapy Is a Human Science

Much Madness is divinest sense—
To a discerning Eye—
Much Sense—the starkest Madness.

Emily Dickinson

When I was a student first entering college, in a burst of youthful enthusiasm, I had the thought that the psychotherapy of severe mental illness offered an opportunity to discover the secrets of the human mind and the depths of human nature. I have had the good fortune to actually devote my life to this quest, and the chapters in this book bring together some of the things that have emerged in the course of nearly 50 years working in the field.

I cannot claim that my journey has unveiled the mystery of the psyche, but I can say it has led to ideas and understandings that, to me anyway, seem interesting. The material develops in the form of a series of thought trains covering important clinical experiences and associated theoretical and philosophical reflections on the nature of the psychotherapy process.

THE CASE OF GRACE

Every psychotherapist has one early case that shapes his or her destiny as a clinician. The following account tells the story of a woman from whom I learned about psychosis, and about what is required of a therapeutic experience in order that the patient's devastation be addressed and healed. The work occurred as part of a postdoctoral fellowship in clinical psychology at Western Missouri Mental Health Center in Kansas City, Missouri, from 1969 to 1972. What made this institution of interest to me was that its director of clinical training was Austin Des Lauriers, a renowned psychotherapist and author of *The Experience of Reality in Childhood Schizophrenia* (1962). Des Lauriers was my clinical consultant in the unfolding of the experiences described.

First, a word about my initial encounter with the patient, a 28-year-old woman whom I shall call Grace. Early one morning—it was 3 a.m.—she came into the screening clinic at the hospital where I was being trained, shouting, and carrying on. Her hair was disheveled, her eyes were wide with excitement, and perspiration drenched her clothes. She demanded to see someone important. I presented myself as that person and sat down to hear her story. A few hours earlier, Grace had experienced an invasion of her bedroom by dazzling flashes of golden light, and she said the flashes had also somehow penetrated into her body. I asked her what she thought this event was. She answered, in loud tones: "I had sexual intercourse with Jesus Christ!… I am filled with His energy, and I am about to *bust!*" For many years, the patient had carried the diagnosis: schizophrenia, paranoid type—*DSM-II*: 295.3. She fulfilled all the criteria: clear signs of thought disorder, inappropriate affect, hallucinations, delusions of grandeur.

Under Des Lauriers' guidance, I arranged to have daily meetings with the patient. I saw her five days a week. She was placed on phenothiazine therapy, and while the drugs certainly slowed her down, they seemed to have no effect on the religious delusions she expressed. Her delusional life was quite involved, and in the early months of my work with her I made an effort to become acquainted with its full extent. I also collected a detailed history from her and from various family members.

She was deeply entangled with God, the Catholic Church, and a special destiny she envisioned for her life on our planet. She considered herself to be the earthly incarnation of the Holy Spirit, a member of the Trinity, and saw her role as one of exercising a peace-making force upon the world as a prelude to the Second Coming of Christ and the End of the World.

From a logical point of view, this patient's delusions were inconsistent with one another in a number of respects, but if one looked at them symbolically, one could discern the presence of repeating themes. She envisioned herself as a member of the Holy Trinity, incarnated to help bring about the coming of our Lord and Savior, setting the stage for her ascension into everlasting life in heaven and the resurrection and salvation of all humanity. She believed that God the Father and God the Son had also taken on earthly form and were present in two individuals of her personal acquaintance. God the Father, she said, resided inside the Bishop of her diocese, a man for whom she had worked as a church volunteer in earlier years of her life. God the Son, Jesus Christ Himself, was present in another man who had served as her counselor during her late teen years. This person, also a devoted Catholic, had tried to help my patient with some very dark depressions that came upon her as a young woman. She had developed great love for this counselor, but their relationship ended when she was 19 and suddenly became psychotic. Although she had not seen him for almost a decade, she looked forward to a joyful reunion within the Trinity at the End of the World.

My patient seemed to entertain fantasies that she might be pregnant, often crying out in the mornings: "I feel nauseated, and I am in pain!" One day, I impulsively responded to this statement by telling her not to worry, because she was not pregnant. She reacted with gales of laughter. Although she never made overt claims to being the mother of Christ, it was apparent that she was identifying with the Holy Virgin. She also believed she had a personal relationship with the Holy Father in Rome, often experiencing vivid hallucinatory flights through the sky to the Vatican, where she would descend from above and be gently deposited upon the lap of the pope. The College of Cardinals, according to her further explanations, was giving consideration to canonizing her, and she eagerly awaited a proclamation from Rome that her sainthood had been declared.

Let me now turn to what I came to understand as a pivotal tragedy that occurred during her childhood. She suffered the experience of what is probably the single most injurious thing that a parent can do to a child: the suicide of her deeply beloved father. It took place when she was 10 years old, shattered her mother and really her whole family—there were also two brothers—and she had no one to help her deal with its cruel aftermath. One afternoon, without any warning, her father had slashed his wrists and hanged himself from a tree.

An event such as this is indescribably destructive. In addition to constituting a traumatic loss, suicide retroactively invalidates the relationship the child had believed in prior to the death. Because it is a willful act, something the parent has chosen to do, a statement has been made as to the significance of the child to that parent. So the very reality of the child's world is attacked by a parent's suicide. All that was believed to be true has been suddenly rendered meaningless; faith in one's own perceptions and thinking is therefore assaulted, and the child is left with the knowledge, never before considered even as a possibility, that he or she was not worth living for. A child having undergone such an experience is in need of very significant support in finding a way to survive what has happened that will not progressively destroy his or her life. But generally the other family members are so traumatized by the death that they are completely unavailable to each other, and this greatly compounds and complicates the situation. All of these things came into play in my patient's early years.

How did Grace go from the tragedy of her father's death to membership in the Holy Trinity? How does someone move from a devastating loss to a messianic destiny to bring on the End of the World (Atwood, 1978)? As I listened to my patient's sad story, I wondered about these things. One could never ask her such questions, though, because in her delusions she was not able to have any kind of ordinary conversation. Whenever the topic of these ideas came up in our meetings, she quickly became carried away with excitement and filled up with feelings of godlike power. If I was unwise enough to ask, for example, why she thought her counselor was the reincarnation of Jesus Christ—and in the early going I often asked very ill-considered questions—she would bound out of her chair and cry out: "I am the Truth, I am the Way, I am the Light, or the suffering, the sorrow, the *pain*, it is the *human* side of Jesus Christ, not the *divine!*" I learned to avoid such direct inquiries into the details of her religious life, and for short periods in our initial meetings I found it possible to engage her in fairly coherent discussions of her childhood background and of very concrete aspects of her program in the hospital.

The answer to the question as to how she went from the father's death to her delusions and hallucinations concerns the pathway she tried to find in the years following the tragedy. It was a pathway of inwardness, of secret prayer, of an attempted drawing close to God, of seeking comfort in the arms of Jesus. She made a kind of pact with her Savior: If He would accept her into a state of rescuing union with Him, she would transform herself and become a purely spiritual being. Telling no one living of her secret commitments, Grace tried to enact the planned union with God by entering a convent at age 17, with the idea of becoming a nun and a missionary and devoting the remainder of her earthly existence to works of self-sacrifice on behalf of the poor and the sick. She tried mightily, as an aspect of this striving toward oneness with her God, to purge herself of every trace of self-interest and personal need, including the whole of her emerging sexuality. She was unable to complete the course of study at the convent, however, and after a year of struggle collapsed into a black depression. This was the time at which she began to receive counseling from a man who was a member of her church and who worked with many priests and nuns.

I am not going to go into the details of their sessions together, although she did describe them fully to me. Suffice it to say that she latched on to her counselor as her Savior, and without telling him what she was thinking began to entertain the notion that at last she had found Jesus—that a miracle had appeared in her life and her counselor was himself the Lord her God. But the spiritual attraction and joy she felt on having at last arrived in His presence was disturbed by other feelings: A confusing, dismaying sexual intensity began to color her tie to her counselor, and she was unable to suppress longings for physical, erotic contact with him. She also began to feel that he was not listening to her and, in spite of his exalted status as a quasi-deity, that he did not care about her suffering. Never saying anything directly regarding these matters, one day, without warning or explanation, she arose in his office and shouted out these words: *"Jesus Christ abandoned me!"*

Following this announcement, Grace walked out and their meetings were discontinued. A few days later she was hospitalized for the first time, already deeply immersed in the delusional fantasies that were present when I first became acquainted with her. Her counselor made no effort to contact her, and she made none to find him. There was nevertheless the fluctuating idea present in her mind that in him she had found God.

Over the course of the next 6 years, Grace went back and forth between relative stability and states of deep religious preoccupation. There were at least 10 separate hospitalizations during this period, some of them lasting months in duration. Finally, shortly after her 28th birthday, in the midst of the latest resurgence of her hallucinations and delusions, she and I found each other.

I spent a lot of time with her, visiting her almost every day for the first 6 or 7 months, sometimes for as long as 2 hours. I could see in the course of these meetings that she was becoming very attached to me—I always found her eagerly waiting when I arrived at the hospital each morning, and she was the last to say goodbye when I left in the evening. There was, however, no particular improvement that was visible as the streaming of her religious fantasies continued, sometimes becoming so intense as to preclude any meaningful conversation. Often she behaved in an imperious manner, barking out orders about what she wanted me to do for her, and promising that if I would comply she would repay my efforts by raising my consciousness and helping me become a spiritually powerful person in my own right. She once stared deeply into my eyes and cried out: "Doctor! I am going to raise you up, from here [*gesturing toward her knees*] to *here* [*raising her hands high over her head and shouting*]!" She became intolerant of any response I made to her words that did not seem to her connected with whatever she was trying to convey, many times angrily screaming out: "Stop cutting me off, you're cutting me off, *stop cutting me off!*"

Such moments were extremely difficult, to say the least, especially because the ideas she was expressing were almost always matters of barely comprehensible, often incoherent religious revelations. In addition to her words, she presented a series of paintings she had completed some time before. These were chiefly concerned with religious themes (e.g., the Crucifixion, the Resurrection, the Holy Virgin, etc.), but others displayed images of fire and destruction, with the words "I AM PAIN," "I AM ANGER," or simply "I AM," scrawled across the canvases in large capital letters.

One day, many months into our relationship, she informed me that there was a secret project she had been working on for more than 2 years that was now on the threshold of completion. I asked her what this project entailed, and she answered, again shouting: "My plan to reach my gold!" At first I did not understand her words, and I asked: "Your goal?" She then roared: "My goallllllll...d!"

Seeming to condense the words *goal* and *God*, this plan involved, as I learned with great difficulty, a program of clandestine meditations and prayer she had developed that were producing healing, loving effects sweeping across the world. She was channeling, via the meditations, God's love, which then was being transmitted to all humanity. The purpose of this was to bring about world peace, and also to create the conditions for the Second Coming of Christ and the End of the World. In order for the plan to be executed, she imagined it would be necessary for her to have a reunion with her old counselor, the man she had identified as Christ on Earth. Following their coming together, the two of them would then join with the Bishop and ascend into Heaven in a burst of radiant glory as the Trinity. The End of the World could then unfold, the souls of all mankind would stand in Judgment, and the Final Ascension of all into Heaven could then take place. "Reaching my gold" meant achieving union with God, the deity that had come to her many months before in the form of miraculous golden light. The patient then gave her instructions: "I want you to call Dr. S., my old counselor, and arrange for me to meet with him. *You will do this!*"

When I at first hesitated in the face of this demand, expressing doubt as to its wisdom, she furiously responded: "*Listen up, you! If you want to know me and be associated with me, you will be a part of my plan and do as I say! Now!*"

This was the crisis point in our evolving relationship: I had been given a choice between participating in her journey and following her orders, or refusing and therefore dropping out of her life. I found her to be almost irresistibly forceful in presenting this demand and was very unsure as to how to respond. I managed to put her off by promising to give her my answer the next day.

By this time, we had spent more than 120 hours together, increasingly, it seemed to me, immersed in her passionate religious expressions. One day when I was playing a game of pool with another patient, she burst into the game room, pushed us out of the way, and held the white cue ball high in the air. She cried out: "*This is the Holy Ghost!*" She then shot the cue ball with great power, and showed intense satisfaction as a number of the balls flew off the pool table.

On another occasion, following a very difficult 2-hour conversation with me on various religious topics, she ran into a room where other patients were playing a game of bingo. Standing before them, she announced in loud tones: *"Lord I am cured! Lord I am saved! Lord I am joy! Do you know who has saved me? That wonderful man, Dr. A. Whooopeeee!"*

Some very serious thinking occurred the night following her instructions regarding the planned reunion with her old counselor. This included a short consultation with the gentleman at the hospital who had been guiding my work, Austin Des Lauriers, who believed psychotherapy was the most important of all things in the treatment of schizophrenia. He suggested standing up to her demands with a countering firmness, one that would more fully establish my presence in her world as the ground of her eventual healing and recovery. He thought that all her extravagant orders and threats were bids for a strength outside herself that she could finally rely on, and that it was up to me to help her find that strength in the connection she and I had been building now for many months. Des Lauriers told me it was time for me to rise and shine.

The next day, I saw her in the late afternoon, and this time our meeting was a very different experience, for both of us. When we sat down and she was about to launch into her Plan and its associated instructions, I stopped her by asking her to be quiet and listen to some things I had to say. When she shouted I was "cutting her off," I answered that I was not; furthermore, now she was the one doing the cutting off, and she needed to stop and listen to me instead. Finally she was silent. I spoke the following words, trying to use a calm but very firm voice.

We have been spending time with each other for days and weeks and months, and I have listened to everything you have told me very carefully. Now I have something to say to you, and you must hear this clearly. There has been a lot of talk about a plan. I want you to know that I have a new plan now, a plan for you, and in my plan you are going to get well, and you will be able to return from the hospital and be with the people who love you. In terms of any meetings to be arranged, there are to be no meetings with anyone except for the ones between you and me, because it is in our work together that the plan I am telling you about will be fulfilled.

> There is only one person on this earth you need to be concerned
> about seeing. I am that person.

She tried at first to interrupt me as I gave this little speech,
but each time she did so I stopped her and insisted again that
she hear what I had to say. Then I repeated the presentation
in somewhat different words. This had to occur perhaps three
times. Finally she objected no more and, after a short period
of silence, began to cry. I had never seen her cry before this
moment. She cried and cried, and then she cried some more.
Half an hour passed, and, finally, she said: "Thank you. I am
leaving now."

The next day I came into the hospital, curious and worried
about what had transpired as a result of our encounter. My patient
was not there; somehow she had persuaded the hospital staff to
give her a pass to spend the day at home with her mother. I called
her home to see what was occurring, and the mother, whom I had
met and spoken to many times, said to me:

> Doctor, what did you do? My daughter is herself again! She came
> home this morning and sat with me, drinking tea on the porch,
> and catching up on the latest news and gossip about our neigh-
> bors. What has happened? She is herself! She is the girl I used to
> know who disappeared a long time ago! This is a miracle!

I saw the patient soon after these developments, and was aston-
ished to find someone completely sane, very interested in the
everyday world and without a trace of the religious preoccupations that had dominated her life and thinking now for many
years. She spoke of interests in leaving the hospital, getting a job,
and helping her mother in taking care of the house where she
lived. It was shocking to witness this change. Overnight, as an
apparent effect of 30 minutes of conversation, a raging paranoid
schizophrenia, a volcano of florid symptomatology, had disappeared and been replaced by a perfectly normal person. I have
never been able to see the phenomena of psychosis in the same
way again. It also helped me to recognize that those who say

so-called schizophrenia cannot be helped by psychotherapy don't know what they are talking about. One needs to have experiences like this in order to learn what is and is not possible.

Grace did fall back a number of times, sometimes violently, again becoming swept away in the religious imagery and the expectations of union with God in Heaven. In each instance, though, I reiterated my little spiel, with continuing good effects on her. She was able to leave the hospital a few weeks later, and in the ensuing years did well. She needed my support for a long period, and, during the first year following our breakthrough, often responded to me as if I myself possessed some sort of miraculous power and enormous significance. I did not comment on such attributions, because I thought they reflected her dependence on our connection as her shattered personal universe was in the process of being reassembled. But she really asked for very little. It was kind of odd that once I established the omnipotent plan I had for her, I didn't have to do much of anything other than remain emotionally available. I watched her in the years afterward come into her own as her initial extreme dependence on our frequent contacts gradually diminished. I also saw her contend with the awful legacy of her father's decision to end his life. She spoke to me and to her family members at great length regarding her sadness and furious anger with him for choosing to kill himself. She did well for the next 30 years, but died suddenly as a result of a cardiac infarction at age 58.

The ending of the story is especially sad because Grace was one of the best people I have ever known. I had contact with her, sometimes sporadic, throughout the remaining years of her life, and I can say she was a joy to her family and friends. She loved animals and was instrumental in rescuing a great many dogs and cats. She remained a deeply religious Catholic, attending mass almost every day. This world would be a better place if there were more such people.

Reflections on Grace's Case

In its simplest terms, the impact of this clinical experience concerned my learning to view the phenomena of so-called psychosis as relative to a certain situational context, rather than as arising solely from a pathological process occurring somehow inside the patient. My understanding was that my patient had been seeking a response from her world to help her deal with the devastation flowing primarily from her father's suicide. Although I did not tell this part of the story earlier, when she was young she had tried to find help from her mother, her brothers, her teachers, and her priest. Her family members had closed down as a consequence of their own very profound trauma, and no one outside her family understood her cries for help. The abandonment space into which her life had fallen created the setting within which she turned to the Son of God. Having been deserted by her father, her family, and, from her point of view, everyone else, she looked for what she needed outside and beyond the world, to her Father in Heaven. Again, however, her unfolding journey through her teen years was punctuated by repeating abandonment shocks, as all her efforts to bring God into the heart of her being did not succeed and instead were rewarded only by a deepening loneliness and despair. These were the conditions within which a spiraling into a delusional reconstruction of a shattered personal world occurred.

Then comes the part of the story in which I was involved. When I finally recognized the importance of standing up to her imperious grandiosity, and found a way to do so that would help her see she was in the presence of someone she could depend on, the destructive course of events in her life began to turn around. Having discovered what she needed in our developing connection, the delusions and hallucinations receded. Very gradually, in the crucible of her initially extreme dependence, the healing process that had been aborted years earlier in her life now had a chance to occur.

Grace's "symptoms," therefore, were not just outward signs of an inward illness; they were reactions to an ongoing experience of continuous abandonment and devastation at the hands of an uncomprehending world—they were desperate cries for help. It occurred to me that perhaps all the symptoms we see in the most severe ranges of so-called mental illness are analogously embedded in contexts of felt unresponsiveness, misunderstanding, and never-ending retraumatization. Such an idea leads to a far more optimistic view of these conditions as to the possibility of some sort of recovery. Maybe, I thought, an understanding of this could inspire us to rethink the problem of psychotherapy for our most extreme cases.

"SO-CALLED" SCHIZOPHRENIA: THE CASE OF ANNA

Whenever I use the word *schizophrenia*, I have found myself prefacing it with the words *so-called*. The experience with Grace, and many analogous ones with other subsequent patients, has led me to this way of speaking. The term *schizophrenia*, meaning "split-mind," was coined 100 years ago by the Swiss psychiatrist Eugen Bleuler (1911/1950), who hoped to reinterpret the field of psychopathological phenomena previously grouped under the label *dementia praecox*. In one respect, this new diagnostic label was an advance over the older language: It highlighted an experience of the splitting apart of one's sense of personal identity, a subjective catastrophe one sees often enough in those patients to whom this diagnosis becomes applied. One of my patients offered the original translation "torn soul," reflecting her own feeling of inner fragmentation. So the diagnostic system has moved in the direction of the patients' phenomenology, which has to be counted as progress. But the word *schizophrenia* is a weird-sounding term, and unless one knows Greek, its roots are obscure. What happened is that it became reified, imagined as the name of an internal illness in mental patients, and then psychiatrists' thinking became captive to their newest brainchild. Today, when we pronounce someone schizophrenic, that unfortunate soul is regarded as a defective, deficient, and disordered being, suffering from a dreadful illness arising from within. I resist such attributions, and so I speak of "so-called" schizophrenia. In my own clinical practice, I never use the term.

I had an experience with a very disturbed young woman, Anna, which contributed to my thoughts on this matter. She was a 19-year-old who had already been hospitalized for a number of years, and my work with her eventually spanned several decades. There was a central delusion in this case concerning a vicious persecution to which she had become subject. She believed evil "death rays" were emerging from the eyes of her enemies, and these rays crossed space and impacted against her face. Then they turned into tiny spinning, drilling machines that bored through her skin and skull, finally reaching the soft neural matter deep within. The persecuting rays/machines produced at her brain's center a hardening, almost like a calcification, and the solidified tissues stopped her from having thoughts or feelings and made her feel she was dying. The deadly action of the rays was countered, however, by a special program of meditations Anna had instituted—intense mental focusing that "dissolved" the inner solidifications and freed her thinking and supported her feeling of being alive. She further explained that once the last solid particles in her nervous system were dissipated, she would undergo a breathtaking transformation she described as becoming "born." The human world was (according to her) divided into the born and the unborn, and she intended, with my help, to become one of the "born ones." I was, she declared, certainly one of the born ones myself, and I was the individual selected by destiny to be her greatest "birth guard."

It required a number of weeks to become familiar with the persecutory delusion and its details; Anna was mostly mute during this period of our work, quietly pursuing her meditations and explaining nothing to anyone. Once the awful experience with which she struggled finally emerged, the difficulty continued and grew harder still. I could not understand what she was talking about with all the references to birth, rays, machines, solidifications. Responding to this lack of comprehension, she began to experience the death rays as flowing out of my eyes as well. We had a series of meetings in which she would cry out: "Please, stop them [*the rays*]! They are killing me! I am dying! Oh God, George, you are killing me! Going, going, going…gone!" At such moments, all communication ceased, as she turned away and refused to speak to me any further. At the next meeting, however, I would be given another chance.

Because I did not understand the symbolism of her delusion at first, I am sure I showed my lack of comprehension in my eyes as she desperately tried to express the ongoing crisis of her life. This situation began to attack her, and she begged me again and again to make the rays stop. I had been drawn into her delusion, as often occurs with such patients; but this does not mean that the possibility of a therapeutic outcome is lost. The therapist who has become the destroyer of souls might also turn out to have the power for their resurrection.

What helped us in getting through the impasse was a dream that Anna reported, one that occurred after a visit in the home of her mother. She dreamt she was standing before a tall mirror, looking down a long, tunnel-like hallway. At the other end of the tunnel, her mother appeared, with a loaded revolver. The two of them stood there, facing each other, and slowly the mother raised the pistol and aimed it. A gunshot rang out; the mirror behind Anna shattered into a cloud of tiny, swirling fragments; and Anna vanished. A disembodied voice then intoned the words "but a shadow on the wall, but a shadow on the wall," as a faint silhouette of something indistinct appeared fleetingly.

The dream and the delusion resemble each other if you look at them closely. In both there is a penetrating action from without, and its result is the killing off of my patient, the murder of her soul. The specific context was a short visit she made to her home on a pass from the hospital, to spend time with her mother. Much of this day had been filled with tension as the mother followed her daughter around the house, saying such things as: "Have you taken your medications yet today? The doctors have given you the medicine to help you! You know you are a sick girl, so don't forget your pills!"

This mode of response, replicating the medically oriented treatment that Anna had been receiving in the hospital setting, was experienced as invalidating and discrediting. Anna did not believe she was mentally ill, and when told so, she felt attacked. She was someone of enormous vulnerability and sensitivity, who needed a very concrete mirroring and validation to feel that she was even present and in existence. Being viewed and responded to on the basis of a psychiatric diagnosis—schizophrenia, in this case—made her feel shattered and erased. The delusion symbolized this killing effect in a vision of penetrating rays from others' eyes that caused the petrifaction of her brain and the annihilation of her subjectivity. The dream expressed the killing of the patient's soul in the image of a gunshot and in the vanishing of her body as she underwent a transforming reduction into nothing more than a fleeting shadow.

I responded to Anna's dream by telling her what I thought it meant in simple, concrete terms: "What an awful dream, and what an awful visit it was for you. All the commotion with your mother made you totally blown away." She was happy with these words and dropped the subject of the dream. Whenever I was able to speak to her in a way that connected to what she felt, she would give a little smile and then move on to the next thing.

When Anna told me the dream of the gunshot, and I saw the context of its symbolic violence in her experience of her mother's verbal assaults and invalidations, it helped me to understand the delusion as well. I had the thought then that she had presented the dream as a gift to help me understand her. I realized that when she looked into my eyes and encountered my confusion, she felt invaded and undermined. Seeing my uncomprehending looks, she became an incomprehensible psychiatric object and lost all sense of her own personhood. I understood now as well that she was symbolizing this felt violence in the imagery of the rays and the deadly solidifications. She needed me to acknowledge the violence she was experiencing in a direct way; otherwise it could only continue. Here is what I said:

> My dear, I have something important to say to you and I want you to listen to it very closely. I know that I have been hurting you, and it has been very, very bad. I see it clearly, and I did not before. Please know that I never intended to bring you harm; it has just been that I didn't understand. Now I do. I hope and I pray that you and I will find a way to undo the damage that has occurred.

The rays from my eyes then ceased to flow. In fact, the whole delusion began to recede at this moment, because now she could look at me and know I had caught on to what had been happening to her. That was all that was needed. It is truly incredible how far a little human understanding can go.

To the extent that Anna's "schizophrenia" can be said to have consisted in her delusional thinking, her so-called mental illness here disappeared as a function of a shift in the intersubjective field constituted by our relationship. As in the case of Grace, a psychosis is seen to be relative to a situational context, in this instance one of intrusive, annihilating invalidation.

Another thought about the crisis of Anna's life then arose, stimulated by my friend Michael Gara's interesting suggestion. He offered the idea that the pattern of Anna's delusion concerning the invasive rays and the neural petrifactions replicated the structure of the attribution that is made when one person diagnoses another as exhibiting schizophrenia, especially when this mental illness is assumed to include an underlying neurobiological disorder. In the delusion, rays emerge from the eyes of persecutors and enter into and render the core of Anna's brain inert, lifeless, devoid of subjectivity. In the diagnostic attribution, the expressions of the patient's experiences are ascribed to a physical defect, localized as an internal condition deep within her central nervous system. Could Anna's delusion, I wondered, have originally arisen out of her experience of finding herself relentlessly viewed as a chronic schizophrenic? Was her vision of her persecution a concretizing symbol of her experience of being viewed as crazy? Her astonishingly positive response to my validation of my own destructiveness with her would seem to be consistent with such an interpretation. Was her intersubjective situation prototypical of so-called schizophrenia in our time?

I do not want to give the impression that Anna's struggles were over as a result of this little intervention. Her severe difficulties and vulnerabilities continued for a great many years. The delusion of the rays and the solidifications, however, vanished and never returned. She was eventually able to leave the hospital, where she had spent such a long time, and live with her mother and father.

PSYCHOTHERAPY AS A HUMAN SCIENCE

I was speaking a few years ago to a colleague in clinical psychology at my university, a woman who was the chairperson of my department at the time. She told me that the field of clinical psychology had moved decisively in the direction of "evidence-based treatment," meaning psychotherapeutic methods that have been empirically substantiated as effective. The whole world of psychoanalysis and its derivatives, according to her, had been called into question as alternative approaches—such as cognitive-behavioral therapy—increasingly were proving to be effective. I was unsure how to respond to these claims, because I could see that my colleague would have little sympathy for my viewpoint.

It is difficult for me to see how anyone serious could take such ideas seriously. Cognitive-behavioral therapy, so-called, has two major problems, each of which is very serious. One is the defining term itself: *cognitive-behavioral therapy*. It is almost an oxymoron: *Cognitive* means having to do with thought, while *behavioral* refers to physical activity that has been divested of subjective meaning. Fusing the two terms creates a conceptual muddle from which I can see no escape. That would be the first reason I would not take such a thing seriously.

Secondly, the practitioners of cognitive-behavioral therapy proceed as if it is possible to alter patterns of thinking without attending to the complex historical origins and meanings of those patterns. They try to skip over the hard work of discovering the events and circumstances that shaped the phenomena we encounter as clinicians, and this evasion is obviously problematic. To help a person, one needs to know what has brought that person to the miserable situation in which he or she is found. Cognitive-behavioral therapy, maddeningly, turns its back on such considerations.

Still another problem arises concerning "empirically" substantiating the effectiveness of "methods" of psychotherapy. Is such a thing possible? What do these words even mean? Can there be any conceivable study of one method against another that has the remotest chance of demonstrating anything relevant? How does one measure effectiveness? Are "methods of treatment" like fertilizing agents at an agricultural research station, something we can apply and then quantify and compare the effects of the application? Perhaps someone would answer that an effective method of therapy should at least provide "symptom relief." But then the use of the term *symptom* calls a medical-diagnostic language game into being, one that wreaks havoc with our efforts to describe and conceptualize psychological disturbances. This area of discussion lacks intellectual coherence, and it is a sad commentary on contemporary clinical psychology that it is caught up within it.

The clinicians and researchers currently enjoying popularity in academic circles are latter-day positivists, insisting that one's claims as to the efficacy of psychotherapy need to be tied down to hard, external data of some kind. The day will never come when this will be possible. Psychotherapy is a human science, and as psychotherapists we learn from the narrative accounts that are given of the journeys we undertake with our patients. Principles of interpretation and intervention are inherent in such accounts, and if these principles can be successfully communicated to others working in our field, then knowledge is thereby being disseminated and confirmed. We do our clinical work, and then we tell one another stories about it. The "evidence," if you want to call it that, for something positive having occurred lies inside the stories that are given. Sometimes the accounts are provided by our patients themselves. Read two magnificent, classic books: *I Never Promised You a Rose Garden* (Greenberg, 1964) and *Autobiography of a Schizophrenic Girl* (Sechehaye, 1951). These works describe two journeys in psychotherapy that were incontestably effective in helping the patients find new ways to live in this world.

THE FUTURE OF PSYCHOTHERAPY

Let me open our discussion up by asking: What are the great issues that are challenging the field of psychotherapy today? Perhaps one can imagine a future in which scholars and clinicians will look back on our current situation. What will they say were the most significant questions and problems of our present age?

I picture future scholars looking back upon us as having created the foundation for a new golden age of psychotherapy practice, one that fulfills the latent potential of our field. I am aware that this idea is based on what many would say is blind hope. There are different aspects to it. One emerging theme in our field has to do with a growing attention to phenomenology, and a receding of extrinsic standards against which human lives are measured. A second aspect pertains to an extension of clinical practice to the most severe ranges of psychological disturbances. And a third is about what philosophically inclined analysts sometimes refer to as the "subjectivity" and "intersubjectivity" of our understanding and practice (Atwood & Stolorow, 1993; Stolorow, et al., 2002).

First, let's take phenomenology. Imagine a world of psychiatry and psychology that has escaped the hegemony of the medical model, one that grounds itself in the study of human lives as they are lived and experienced. The diagnostic systems we know today are based on an assessment of so-called symptoms, which are defined by their status as departures from a preestablished standard of normality or mental health. Imagine a diagnostic framework that instead groups individual worlds of experience according to the content and themes that they show.

The word *diagnosis*, etymologically understood, means a separating and a knowing. I am speaking of worlds of individual experience that can be known and studied. One sees certain resemblances and certain differences. Placing a descriptive word to indicate the similarities does nothing more than point out their presence. So one can note, for example, that some worlds are marked by a theme of personal annihilation, manifest in repeating experiences of being erased, rendered into nonbeing. Other worlds show a background of stability and substantiality, but within them there is an objectless foreboding, a feeling of being menaced but without any clear focus as to what the threat might be. A third group of worlds, differing from the first two, might be ones in which the personal sense of authenticity has been surrendered in an enslaving pattern of compliance in order to secure otherwise threatened ties to emotionally important others. Noting the presence of these various distinguishing themes and developing a descriptive vocabulary for them places no one in a box and does not get lost in a system of reified mental illnesses. Imagine a future in which we will have a richly developed phenomenological vocabulary, and a wide and deep base of clinical knowledge about the life-contexts in which the various kinds of experiences encountered come into being and are magnified. Imagine as well the accompanying field of psychotherapy practice, in which our ways of approaching people would be uniquely tailored to the content of the individual world of the person turning to us for help.

In years and decades to come, I see our descendants, looking back, focusing on the best that exists already. This leads to the second of the aspects of my hopeful vision: the extension of psychotherapy practice into the most extreme range of psychological disturbances, those human situations currently grouped together as the so-called psychoses.

Our future counterparts 50 and 100 years hence, as I foresee them, herald the efforts that are being made to devise psychotherapeutic strategies for patients currently labeled psychotic. There have always been people working in our field who have undertaken the most difficult clinical cases—one thinks of Jung (1907), Federn (1953), Sechehaye (1951), Laing (1959), Binswanger (1963), Searles (1965), Des Lauriers (1962), Winnicott (1958), Sullivan (1953), Fromm-Reichmann (1954), Semrad (1980), Karon and VandenBos (1994), Karon (2008), among others. But in our current world, such efforts are still the exception, and the consensus is that psychotherapeutic intervention in the psychoses—in particular in what is called schizophrenia and bipolar disorder—is an enterprise destined for failure. In the more enlightened age that is to come, if my hope turns out to be fulfilled, such views will be widely regarded as without foundation.

We will be seen as mostly having lived in a dark age, but one sprinkled with points of light. The whole way of conceptualizing psychological disturbances will shift away from the ideas of illness and disorder, and toward the specific human experiences that are involved. We will speak of crises, catastrophes, and chronic dilemmas, and not of dysfunction and disease. Those things understood as symptoms of pathology will become reinterpreted as symbols of emotional disaster and as attempted restorative reactions in the face of extreme trauma. The emphasis, in other words, will become transposed from what is lacking in relation to an imagined ideal of normality, to an immersion in what is present as a lived experience.

Recall the story of the young woman with whom this chapter began, Grace. Her admission to the hospital where I met her was occasioned by a set of visions: Golden light had flooded into her bedroom and penetrated into her body. She interpreted this infusion as an experience of sexual union with Jesus Christ. Within the older thinking, the reported flashes of light would be regarded as visual hallucinations, symptoms of a psychosis. Our successors, by contrast, will see such experiences as restorative efforts, connected to the tragic circumstances of this young woman's life.

The sexuality was itself a symbol of a coming together, a fusion in which the patient became one with her heart's desire. She was looking toward Heaven in a search for the strength underlying all of creation, and as the golden light flowed into her body and soul, she began to radiate its limitless power herself. It is commonplace in the phenomenology of grief that one identifies with the person one longs for but has lost. An illusion of that person's presence is thereby generated, in his or her features becoming incorporated into oneself. I see the moment in which the divine energy of God became infused into my patient as symbolic of such an identification. It was a process in which she became the God for whom she longed, undoing her tragic losses and repairing her shattered world. Looking at it in this way, our focus is not on the departure of her experiences from our consensual definitions of what is real; instead we orient ourselves to the inner patterns of Grace's life as she was trying to reconstruct it.

To illustrate further this changing focus, let me tell about some persistent auditory hallucinations of one of my other patients, and I will also recount a dream she reported that helped me to understand the meaning of her voices. This was a young woman in the throes of a bitter divorce from an emotionally abusive husband. There were child custody issues, bitter disputes about a financial settlement, and relentless mutual hatred and accusation. As the divorce process moved along and the cycles of attack and counterattack intensified, my patient began to hear voices calling her various insulting names: "She's a bitch from hell! She's a scumbag whore! She's a liar cunt!" A paranoid fantasy began to emerge in which conspirators were working against her and trying to destroy her sanity by broadcasting these awful messages on the radio.

Then she had a dream, which was important in understanding what the critical voices actually represented. In the dream, she stood alone in her home, and there were dozens of birds that had somehow gotten beneath the shingles on the roof, penetrating into the walls and the space above her ceiling. They were flying about and making a tremendous racket. It was immediately apparent to me what these terrifying birds symbolized: The hostility and ugly accusations in her divorce battle were finally getting to her, attacking her self-esteem and usurping the integrity of her sense of who she was. Each bird was one of her husband's disparaging attributions, and the felt pressure of his intensifying hatred was finally throwing my patient into an annihilation state. The attack, symbolized by the incursion of the birds into the very structure of her home, is dealt with in the auditory hallucinations by a kind of reexternalization of the usurping, invalidating opinions. Casting the invaders back into the outside world expresses a need to recover her own boundaries and reestablish the integrity of her own self-experience. The auditory hallucinations and the associated paranoia were thus not symptoms of an illness; they were expressions of my patient's efforts to psychologically survive. This is the kind of thinking I envision as an accepted part of our field in its future development. People working with such ideas now are the points of light our counterparts to come will perceive in the vast darkness of our time.

What was my response to learning of my patient's voices? I told her what I thought they signified: that the divorce battle was getting under her skin. I also told her that there was only one voice she should really be listening to, and this all-important voice was none other than her own. I found that this helped with the hallucinations and the paranoia, which began now to recede. The power of my words was of course based on the emotional depth of my connection to the patient, whom I had worked closely with already for a number of years.

Why did the pressure of this woman's husband's hatred begin to usurp and annihilate her? The vicious attacks by the husband replicated equally vicious emotional assaults the patient experienced as a young child by her mother. She was a survivor of extreme child abuse, and the emotional violence and the invalidations of her early years were reawakened in her disintegrating marriage. When one sees such reactions, there is almost always a current situation having effects that repeat and resurrect an earlier one.

"SO-CALLED" BIPOLAR DISORDER

Among the phenomena we conventionally see as "symptoms" in severe psychological disturbances would be shifting, cycling mood states. Do these also become reinterpreted as restorative as in the case of many hallucinations and delusions?

"So-called" bipolar disorder is, of course, the crowning instance of such shifts and cycles. This quintessentially psychological phenomenon, as I would understand it, has in our time been wrongly ceded to the biological psychiatrists, the reductionists who are true believers in genetic and biochemical origins. Our friends in the future will shake their heads in dismay at the virtually complete disconnect between the medical certainties that are maintained about this matter and the poverty of supporting scientific evidence. There have been, however, points of light in the history of our field that concern the phenomenological basis of this condition.

There was a faint glow in the early observations and interpretations of Melanie Klein (1934), who wrote about this topic. The conflicts belonging to what she called the depressive position were central in her conceptualization, wherein the child suffers in an experience of his or her aggression being dangerous to the survival of the parenting figure. Unfortunately, she was limited by an imprisoning theory of innate drives that obscured her phenomenological insight into what children in the midst of profound enmeshment feel about their own aggressive, self-assertive impulses. I think also of Frieda Fromm-Reichmann (1959), who studied bipolar patients intensively. She concluded that as children they were never treated as distinct persons, but instead were viewed as extensions of their caregivers. Then we have Donald Winnicott (1958), who elaborated the idea of the manic defense—in particular he made the interesting suggestion that mania is a protection against not just depression, but against an underlying state of psychic death. Finally we come to my dear friend Bernard Brandchaft (1993, 2010), who had the luminous idea about manic-depressive patterns that they are concerned with a struggle against the experience of personal annihilation. Put most simply, the meaning of mania, according to him, is that it embodies a transitory liberation from an enslaving, annihilating tie to emotionally important others, whereas the depression into which a manic patient collapses represents the reinstatement of that tie. There may be other pathways to bipolarity, but I have found Brandchaft's ideas abundantly illustrated among the many such patients I have observed.

I consider the psychotherapy of the so-called bipolar patient to be possibly the single most important contemporary frontier of clinical psychoanalytic research, but I cannot say that our knowledge in this area has advanced very far. I will offer a few thoughts that have come to me over the years in which I have given this problem consideration.

THE CASE OF THOMAS

A first idea appeared during a consultation with a colleague some years ago. My associate, a psychologist, sought my advice regarding what she thought was a sudden turn for the worse in a bipolar patient she had been treating for a very long time. This patient, a 45-year-old man whom I will call Thomas, had shown a classic manic-depressive pattern, oscillating violently between the extremes of uncontrolled euphoria and suicidal depression. He had been hospitalized a number of times; there had been serious attempts to kill himself; and he had squandered all his family's money in spending sprees and harebrained investments. My colleague had persisted with this man through a number of these crises, trying to help him basically by just being emotionally available and always maintaining their schedule of psychoanalytic sessions three times each week.

Now, however, in the aftermath of Thomas's latest bout of disruptive mood swings, something else had appeared. The man informed his analyst that he, the patient, had suddenly recognized that he was in absolute control of all his analyst's thoughts. Hearing of this reported mental omnipotence, my colleague concluded her patient was sinking into a delusional state. This was very depressing for her, because she had given of her time and energy to this man for a number of years. I asked her to say more about her patient, about what it had been like to work with him for this long period. Something interesting then appeared.

She told me that his patient's emotional life had always been strangely opaque, almost as if it did not exist. On the first occasion, near the beginning of their meetings, when asked how he was feeling, the patient had been nonplussed. He said no one had ever asked him such a question, and he did not have any idea about what his feelings were. He said he did not know what the word *feelings* even meant. He was familiar with the overwhelming rush of his manic states, and he knew about wanting to die. But he was a man who reported that there was no emotional life otherwise that could be described. He could not introspect or reflect, had no vocabulary for expressing what he experienced, and if pressed on the matter became very upset.

I wondered aloud about whether this absent inner life pertained to a developmental background that was an empathic vacuum, devoid of human understanding and offering nothing to help him develop a language articulating her emotions. This had not occurred to my colleague, who had seen her patient's opaqueness as some kind of congenital peculiarity that needed no further explanation. She confirmed, however, the idea that there had never been any talk about emotions in the patient's family, because the parents had related to their son as a purely exterior being, almost as if they were some sort of strange behaviorists. They focused on his actions, and their approval of him was strictly conditional on whether or not he met their very high standards of conduct. There were indications, according to the psychologist, that the parents' avoidance of their child's inner life pertained to a terror of psychosis on their parts.

Then further questions arose in my mind, especially about Thomas's so-called delusion concerning having absolute control over all his analyst's thoughts. What if, I wondered, this seeming delusion expressed the arrival of a miracle in the patient's world: an experience of actually commanding the attention of another human being? What if the absence of an emotional life was the secondary effect of missing empathy, of profoundly absent emotional attunement in his family of origin? Maybe no one ever took the time to sit down and listen to him. A child who is never listened to is subject to annihilation.

What if, I continued to ask, this man grew up among people who saw him as the normal, conventional child they needed him to be instead of the one he actually was? What happened then to the person he might otherwise have become? My answer: That person may have vanished, almost without a trace, as a life unfolded in a structure of compliance that embodied an identity borrowed from his caregivers' expectations.

Sometimes such a situation eventuates in an anorexic pattern, wherein the experience of the deprivation of emotional attention is symbolized in the repeating acts of self-starvation. The sense of agency that is given up in conforming to parental pressures and becoming the child that is wanted and approved of, in anorexia, reappears in an active refusal of the intake of nourishment. There the exercise of absolute control over what physical substances pass into the body stands in contrast to the passive compliance in which the child surrenders to being authored by the external human surround. Here again we see something conventionally regarded as a symptom of an illness that is better understood as an expression of a will to exist and survive. Obviously there is also a paradox, in that the agentic self-assertion implicit in the anorexic starvation project also often brings about biological death.

In other instances, as in the case of the patient about whom I was being consulted, a manic-depressive cycle springs into being, one in which the positions of surrender through compliance and of rebellion and protest alternate with each other. Keeping all of this in mind, the idea the patient evinced that he had absolute control over his analyst's thoughts could be considered an amazing breakthrough, a first form of an experience of attunement heralding the possibility of an emotional life arising that belongs to the patient and that could result in a freedom from the deadly cycles of bipolarity.

I suggested to my colleague that she seek ways of validating, mirroring, and really celebrating the experience Thomas was now having of being in command of his thoughts. I told her that this feeling, being so utterly new, must also be a tenuous and unstable sort of thing, and that perhaps the need to hold on to this emergent sense was causing him to concretize and elaborate it in a seeming delusion. Unfortunately, she was unable to follow my advice, focusing instead on the disparity between her patient's new claims of omnipotence and the content, as she saw and defined it, of objective reality. A battle ensued between the two of them, and the opportunity to support the patient's apparent development was lost. I was told my advice made no sense, because it is not good clinical practice to encourage delusional thinking. She chose instead to interpret her patient's imagined control as a wish fulfillment, counteracting the effects of their separations between sessions of the psychotherapy. Thomas rejected this idea, and ceased to speak of controlling his therapist's mind.

I was able to follow up on this case a few years later when I had an opportunity to contact my colleague again. I asked her what had occurred in the period subsequent to the episode regarding which I had provided a consultation. She said that in the months following the remarkable claim of mental control, her patient had repeatedly accused her of trying to make him conform to some standard model of mental health, much as his parents had tried to mold him into an ideal child. A dream the patient presented at the time seemed to symbolize his struggle. In that dream he was being pursued by a gang of shadowy, frightening figures as he climbed the stairs to his psychologist's office. They seemed to be vampires, and they intended to kidnap and kill him. After a period of a year, Thomas abruptly terminated his sessions with his therapist.

My colleague, in interpreting the patient's seeming delusion, followed in the spirit of Freud's (1924) understanding of psychotic states as involving a turning away from a frustrating external reality in favor of a substitute imaginary world in which irresistible desires are fulfilled. Offering such an idea invalidates emergent modes of experience that, on account of being new and unstable, become cast into a language of concretizing symbols. So often the potential to move beyond the place of one's injury and imprisonment is subverted by the blinding certainties of those to whom one turns for help.

Nevertheless, I think it would be worthwhile to pursue the sort of thing this case presented. Perhaps other patients, followed intensively for long enough, could develop in a similar way, and one could discover whether an aborted developmental process could then be reinstated within the medium of the patient's experience of his or her therapist's empathy. This would require great dedication and long periods of time. One would have to be prepared to live through the crises, do what one could to avert the patient's complete self-destruction, and then hope that the needed underlying connection of empathy and validation could crystallize. People in our field today want quick results, so they turn to electroconvulsive therapy, lithium carbonate, and the like. In the golden age of psychotherapy that is to come, it will be understood that genuine healing is not likely to come quickly.

THE CASE OF MARY

Some related thoughts arise out of more recent efforts I have made to help a young woman, whom I will call Mary, who also carried a bipolar diagnosis. She had experienced, in her late teens and early 20s, a number of manic episodes, requiring hospitalizations and eventuating in a high number of electroconvulsive treatments (ECT). She came to me when she and her family began to see that the ECT was having a devastating impact on her memory and cognitive functioning.

I was interested in Mary's description of the experience of her most recent mania. She explained that the chaos of her adult life had never bothered her much, because she had relied instead on the treasures of her own mind, on the fascinating intricacies of her rich imagination. She had been able always to escape her oppressive life situations—for example, of being a college student unable to complete her studies, or of being a young woman who was fast becoming a terrible disappointment to her parents—by turning to fantasy, to thrilling, exhilarating images of herself and her life in a world apart from this one. The problem was that when she gave herself over to this alternative reality, she also lost all control of her own thoughts and feelings. Glorious plans and dreams of unparalleled grandeur would materialize, and when she then was driven to enact these, disaster would occur, with hospitalization following along soon thereafter. As we spoke, I learned that she had, in her younger years, tried mightily to please her parents and other authorities, striving always for perfection and success. She had in fact become a slave to the goal of being a perfect golden child.

As she suffered under this imprisonment in her late teens, however, in the context of a series of disorienting changes and losses in her personal situation, a wonderful universe of freedom suddenly opened up before her mind, one she plunged into with joyful enthusiasm. This was a realm of liberation she had never known, and its intoxicating power became irresistible.

But then her newly crystallized plans and dreams led to catastrophe, and she was subjected to hospitalization, antipsychotic medications, and electroshock therapy. The child who had existed earlier and who had sought to please her family reappeared. Back and forth she went over the next several years, between uncontrolled manic highs and conformist depressive lows, and her electroconvulsive treatments and her lithium ultimately could not stop these oscillations, or they did so only at the expense of the functioning of her own mind. Then she and her family found their way to me.

I asked Mary what she wanted. She answered that she wanted to live for herself. That became the theme of our connection. She complained of there being "voices," haunting, whispering presences that criticized and devalued her in every situation she encountered. I told her, as is my habit in such cases, that there was only one voice she should pay attention to: that would, of course, be just her own. She sat with that declaration for a moment or two, and then said to me: "You are a practitioner of 'I-therapy,' aren't you? You seem like you are all for 'I.'" I answered that indeed I was one who believed in "I," and regarded "I" as sacred and therefore to be protected and honored in every way possible. The young woman seemed at this point to relax in my presence, and told me much more about the voices she heard and the siren-call of the images that embodied freedom and glory.

A shared understanding seemed to appear in our long discussions of her adventures over the previous years of her life, one in which her extreme mood swings were viewed as alternations between trying to be perfect and pleasing to others on the one hand and seeking profound emancipation from such efforts on the other. The lure of the manic states was very strong, always promising to deliver wonderful gifts, but leading in every instance to disaster. The depressions following her highs were very severe, filled with the critical voices, and often provoking a suicidal despair. She and I said to each other that the key to her recovery would be found in the achievement of a new balance between these polarized alternatives, an equilibrium that would not be one of perfection and that also would not require or involve infinite freedom. She said, and I agreed, that only she could establish and maintain this balance. She also suggested a metaphorical image for my role as her psychotherapist in this endeavor in search of a new personal center: I was to be her lighthouse, a point of reference in the night and, in whatever storms might arise, one to which she could look in advancing her journey toward stability.

I have only known Mary for a few years. She has had her ups and downs in this period, but we have succeeded in avoiding any further ECT. In the meantime she continues to experience her therapy as a lighthouse, one that helps keep her "I" on its pathway, and we are hopeful that over time the stable life she seeks will become hers. I am thinking we will need at least a decade in this process, so we shall see.

Mary has increasingly assimilated my presence in her life as an ally and resource for the support of her sense of "I-ness," and I think this would be an indispensable precondition for the successful treatment of the so-called bipolar patient. Without a connection that is felt to be sustaining and supporting in this way, the psychotherapist can only be seen as an agent of society, one of the forces pushing the patient in the direction of normality and compliance. That is a recipe for psychological death in the lives of such people, who will then be condemned to the manic-depressive cycles without end.

Something has happened in the lives of bipolar patients to sever the connection between accommodative and individualizing trends in their personalities. In mania we see a roman candle shooting out the fires of pure freedom and uniqueness. In the depressions that ensue, one witnesses the extinction of the flames of liberty, as the darkness and despair of surrender to the agendas of family and society rush in. Something needs to occur to mend the rift that has opened up in the core selfhood of the patient, something that will bridge the two stark alternatives and establish a stability free of the bipolar swings. This something is the work of the therapy, and it can only occur as a result of the patients' own volitions. The effort of this work, in turn, can only be sustained in the facilitating presence of an other who can be a lighthouse for the journey. This would be an example of the principle that the "I" can only come into being in relation to an answering and orienting "Thou" (Buber, 1923/1970).

The pathway of the journey will often involve creative works in some way. The act of creation, in all areas of art and literature and philosophy, offers abundant opportunities for integrating conflicting currents in our natures, for bridging rifts that have opened up in the warfares of bipolarity. My patient Mary, for example, made great strides in pulling herself together in a developing career in modern dance. Others I have known or studied found in poetry their pathways toward unification, or in musical composition, or in the elaboration of interesting, integrative philosophical doctrines. This is an area in which there needs to be continuing studies of all the ways people find to heal their fractured souls (Atwood et al., 2011). Extensive knowledge of such matters, in turn, will prepare clinicians for their sacred roles as lighthouses in the stormy travels of the patients who turn to them for help. We are still at the beginning of the long process of developing this knowledge.

THE PLACE OF THE THERAPIST

This third aspect of what I hope I am seeing in the contemporary development of our field has to do with the radical engagement of the person of the therapist in whatever process of psychotherapy occurs. What does the term *radical engagement* mean in this context? It means that the therapist, as an individual, is implicated in everything that takes place within the psychotherapeutic dyad. It means that there is no such thing as detached observation. It means that the transformations that occur, if any do, include both participants.

My use of the term *implicated* might seem to indicate that a crime of some sort has occurred. The things that happen in what is called psychotherapy or psychoanalysis often enough are crimes, emotional crimes committed against those we are entrusted to help. But that is not the connotation I want to highlight. It is more the idea that the imprint of the therapist's subjectivity, of his or her personality, is everywhere present in the psychotherapeutic process. Psychotherapy, far from being any sort of procedure that is administered from a place of detachment, is always a dialogue between two personal universes, one that transforms both.

On more than one occasion at psychoanalytic conferences, I have been asked how it is then that we are to distinguish which of the people involved in an analysis is the patient. I become impatient with such questions, and once suggested that one can see which is which by determining which one is crying. Of course, that doesn't work when the patient does something so upsetting that the therapist breaks into tears. A psychotherapeutic dialogue, if it is in any measure successful, always illuminates and transforms the worlds of both of the people involved, and as far as I am concerned, this is actually self-evident.

Consider again my early clinical experience with Grace, my religious patient who visualized herself as part of the Holy Trinity. Her journey of healing utterly transformed my understanding of the whole realm of severe psychological disturbances and of the potential of psychotherapy to address them. Recall her promise that she would raise me up from someone small and weak into a position of strength and power. She certainly succeeded in doing that. I could also speak of the effect of witnessing her struggle with her father's suicide as her mourning process unfolded. I could not follow these developments without a corresponding opening up of my own early experiences of trauma and loss. To see someone coming to the truth of his or her life is, inevitably, to be brought closer to the truth of one's own. In the golden age of psychotherapy practice that is to come, this idea will be axiomatic. All the phenomena of psychotherapy will be understood as taking place within an intersubjective field, one that creates a constitutive context for the experiences and actions of both analyst and patient.

2

Exploring the Abyss of Madness

Things fall apart; the centre cannot hold.

William Butler Yeats

THE GIRL WITH FOUR IMAGINARY CHILDREN IN HER BEDROOM

I saw a 19-year-old woman a great many years ago, hospitalized, who refused to speak except to say that there were four children living in her bedroom. According to her parents, she had been entirely normal, reportedly perfectly delightful in fact, until just a few weeks before, but now she was in prolonged silence. The psychiatrist assigned to her gave her a diagnosis of schizophrenia, and she was begun on a course of antipsychotic medications. Her behavior remained the same: long stretches of silence, very occasionally interrupted by short statements that four children were in her room. She would not describe the children, explain their origin, or otherwise engage in any further communication on the matter. When asked if she believed the children were real, actual human beings, a look passed across her face of confusion and dismay. The doctor, after a period of weeks, recommended shock therapy, and a course of 12 electroconvulsive treatments (ECT) then took place. Following these, she spoke just once to say there were now no children in her bedroom; otherwise the reign of silence continued. Finally, she was discharged and her family took her home. We never saw her again. But I was haunted by what had occurred and always wondered about what happened to the young woman and what her behavior could have meant. In the following, I offer some hypotheses about this patient, and her story becomes a point of departure for a journey into the nature of madness.

Looking back on this experience from the vantage point of all that I have seen since, there are five items that stand out: first, that she was, according to her parents, a "perfectly delightful" child prior to the transformation in her behavior; second, that the primary change was one of lapsing into silence; third, the sporadic statements regarding there being four children sharing her bedroom; fourth, her apparent confusion in response to being asked about whether she believed the children were real; and fifth, following ECT, her report that the children were no longer present in her bedroom.

Let us suppose that the perfectly delightful girl her parents knew her to be was the product of a surrender, rooted in very early experiences of great power, a deep-ranging accommodation in which she brought herself into compliance with agendas as to who she was and should be, transmitted to her by her mother and father. The identity that developed would then be one taken over from preexisting images they supplied, rather than from her emergent agency and spontaneous intentionality. The sudden disappearance of that delightful girl would thus be comprehensible as an act of rejecting the false self, of fighting back against the enslaving tie to the maternal and/or paternal agenda, and therefore an effort to rescue possibilities of her own being from annihilation. I would interpret the silence as a negation of her compliance, wherein the whole field of speech has been co-opted by the conforming trends of her personality, and the only way to oppose them is to stop talking. She stops speaking, but not quite completely. The one little statement that remains is about the four children living in her bedroom. Let us assume that this bedroom is *a room of her own*, a space within which whatever exists or remains of her authentic possibilities can live and survive. Why are there four? Air, earth, fire, and water come to mind—the fundamental elements of the universe. I have read in the Jungian literature that quaternity is a symbol of wholeness. Here, though, one sees not wholeness but fragmentation, a collection of children rather than one coherent personality. Authenticity in the context of extreme pathological accommodation (Brandchaft et al., 2010) is at best a fragmentary, evanescent sort of thing, scarcely organized at all, lacking in the capacity to endure or coalesce. And yet this is what remains of the young woman's soul: four children, living in a room of her (their) own.

From a perspective valuing such authenticity, this young woman's breakdown into silence and delusion might better be considered an attempted *breakthrough*—to a life that, perhaps for the very first time, would actually belong to her. But such a possibility could not become actual without someone there to recognize and give it such a meaning, without a Thou to perceive the I trying to assemble itself out of its fragmentary possibilities.

Then we come to the so-called treatment of this young woman: medications, followed by electricity. The effect of these interventions was finally reflected in her statement that there were no children in the bedroom. This outcome might well be a tragedy, a sign of great and perhaps enduring damage having been done to this young person's chance to somehow pull herself together and have a life that could belong to her.

The apparent bewilderment she seemed to express when asked a question about whether she regarded the children as real also has importance. Of course, the reason such a question would be asked pertains to the issue of her *reality testing*, the question as to whether she was in contact with all that her doctors consider true and real. From her point of view, the question would have to be enormously confusing, for it was her need above all that the children be real. If I am right in my speculations, the reason she concretized the fragmentary state of her soul into the image of actually living children is precisely that she could not, at her center, sustain any sense that she was an actually existing, alive, real person. But she was perfectly smart, and she could see that her psychiatrist would react to any idea that the children were real as a sign of her serious mental illness, perhaps necessitating further drastic medical interventions. So, to say that the children were not real would be to embrace annihilation; but to claim that they were real would be to accept a pathologizing diagnosis and damaging medical intrusions. She was confused for the simple reason that there is no viable journey possible between this Scylla and this Charybdis.

This is a very sad story, and I hope that she arrived in some better situation once her parents took her away from the institution. I would like to think they found a setting for her in which she could perhaps follow an artistic pathway. The journey of creativity is very often one that supports a person's sense of being real. It even occurs to me that one could look at her descent into silence—and what her psychiatrist saw as delusion—as a piece of performance art, affirming her being in a rebellion against her family context and expressing to the world an indomitable life spirit within her. It would be extremely interesting to follow what might have happened had her analyst/psychiatrist taken such an attitude toward her so-called symptoms. I suspect she would have found him or her to be someone she could talk to.

Was this young woman suffering from madness? I would say yes, she was, in that madness is the abyss. Phenomenologically, going mad is a matter of the fragmentation of the soul, of a fall into nonbeing, of becoming subject to a sense of erasure and annihilation. The fall into the abyss of madness, when it occurs, is felt as something infinite and eternal. One falls away, limitlessly, from being itself, into utter nonbeing.

INTO THE ABYSS

My students often ask me my opinion of psychiatry's understanding of madness—of contemporary diagnostic systems with their differentiations and classifications—with a view of the various forms of madness as disorders and diseases. I answer as follows: The ever-proliferating systems of nomenclature in psychiatry are among the field's most serious embarrassments, and nowhere as disturbingly as in the efforts that have been made in the study of madness. The notion of an orderly system that arranges and distinguishes this form and that form of infinite falling, nice little categories of a chaos that is beyond imagining and describing, is preposterous. It is human to try to bring order into disorder, but it is also human to be preposterous. The diagnostic systems that have been and continue to be generated lack all scientific foundation and are actually laughable. I am ashamed to belong to a field capable of such things.

Madness is not an illness, and it is not a disorder. Madness is the abyss. It is the experience of utter annihilation. Calling it a disease and distinguishing its forms, arranging its manifestations in carefully assembled lists and charts, creating scientific-sounding pseudo-explanations for it—all of these are intellectually indefensible, and I think they occur because of the terror. What is the terror I am speaking of? It is the terror of madness itself, which is the anxiety that one may fall into nonbeing.

The abyss lies on or just beyond the horizon of every person's world, and there is nothing more frightening. Even death does not hold a terror for us comparable to the one associated with the abyss. Our minds can generate meanings and images of our deaths: We can picture the world surviving us, and we can identify with those that come later or otherwise immortalize ourselves through our works. We can rage against the dying of the light, and we can look forward to reunions with lost loved ones. We can think about the meaninglessness of human existence and its finiteness. We can be relieved that all our sorrows will soon be over. We can even admire ourselves for being the only creatures in existence, as far as we know, who perceive their own wretched destiny to be extinguished. The abyss of madness offers no such possibilities: It is the end of all possible responses and meanings, the erasure of a world in which there is anything coherent to respond to, the melting away of anyone to engage in a response. It is much more scary than death, and this is proven by the fact that people in fear of annihilation—the terror of madness—so often commit suicide rather than continue with it. Death is a piece of cake compared to the abyss.

I think the reason so many in our society want to think of madness as a disease, perhaps localized in the brain and arising from organic predispositions, is that such ideas soothe the terror of the abyss. One must find some explanation for the extreme claims people in the highest offices of psychiatry make in this connection, because the science to support those claims is not strong, nor will it ever be. The abyss is a potential inhering in every human life, and the dream of contemporary psychiatry is to pin down a tangible source or cause for this potential. Once this is successful, so goes the thinking, some intervention will become possible to eliminate it. It is a dream never to be fulfilled. We are stuck with the abyss as an irreducible possibility of our lives, and we would be better off to understand that. Psychiatry here reminds me of the person who has actually fallen into the abyss and then gone on to develop the idea that there is an "influencing machine" (Tausk, 1917) sending persecutory rays into his or her body and mind. You see, if there is such a machine somewhere, operated by one's enemies, a hope is held out that this machine can be found, turned off, and finally destroyed; and one's malicious adversaries can then be brought to justice and disposed of. The biological sources of the so-called psychoses are miniature influencing machines, located in the molecular structures of who we are, and once these tiny machines are detected, we can turn them off or modify them, or maybe even breed them out of the human race. We as doctors can also reassure ourselves that our own organic constitutions do not include these predispositions, the little molecular machines twisted into our DNA, and we are therefore protected from the abyss. This is all illusion. The abyss is within all of us as a human possibility, forevermore, and so we will never be safe from it.

Am I saying that everyone, all of us, are forever on the threshold of madness? No. I am saying that the abyss is a universal possibility, which is not the same thing as claiming we all are always on its threshold. Most of us spend our lives in a stable and sane worldview that does not bring us, subjectively speaking, to the doorway to madness. Our sense of our own existence and security is steady; in fact, it is such a given part of the bedrock of our lives that we never really think about it. That does not mean, however, that the sanity we enjoy in our cozy little worlds cannot be taken from us. It can, because we all are capable of falling into the abyss. Something might happen, and then the center cannot hold.

Sometimes what happens in the fall into the abyss is that the sustaining events of our lives cease to occur. People often fall not because the bad happens, but rather because the good stops happening. Sanity is sustained by the network of validating, affirming connections that exist in a person's life: connections to other beings. If those links fail, one falls. The beings on whom one relies include, obviously, other people, sometimes animals, often beings known only through memory and creative imagination. In some instances it is the connection to God that protects a person against madness. Strip any person of his or her sustaining links to others, and that person falls. No one is immune, because madness is a possibility of every human life.

It might be asked: If a link to God shields some people from the abyss, why is it that the symptoms of madness so often circle around special relationships to God, delusions sometimes even of being God? One of the problems with such a question is that it speaks of *symptoms*, returning us to a medical and diagnostic viewpoint that cannot be helpful in our task of discovering the human meanings in what is expressed to us. Generally, people claiming to be God or to have a unique connection to the

Almighty are resurrecting a sustaining tie that has been shattered. This was illustrated dramatically in the case of Grace, presented in chapter 1. The so-called delusion re-creates a lost connection to someone life-giving, and thus becomes comprehensible as an attempt to climb back out of the abyss. The signs and symptoms that psychiatry likes to arrange in its orderly diagnostic systems are pretty much efforts to return to sanity from madness.

For example, I once worked with a 7-year-old girl who heard God's voice speaking to her. She was so occupied with her conversations with the Creator that she was neglecting her schoolwork and ceasing to relate to her family members. I found out what had happened. She had been enmeshed to an extreme degree with her mother in her early years, adopting a role of comforting and soothing that helped the mother keep her emotional balance in a marriage that was full of strife. But then the mother became pregnant and had a hospitalization lasting months because of extreme complications of the pregnancy and a very difficult birth. The child was left with her father, to whom she turned then to replace the missing closeness with her beloved mother. Everything went well for the initial weeks, although there was great anxiety as to whether the mother was going to survive and recover. But then the father, evidently, felt sexually deprived by his wife's absence, and a period of molestation followed, eventually culminating in full sexual intercourse with his daughter. The father, who had begun to replace the missing mother, in the sexual acts destroyed himself as anyone this child could rely on. She was eventually able to tell me, in her doll play, how the whole world "went wobbly" after the father's intrusions began, which was her way of saying she had begun to fall into the abyss. But the crisis of wobbliness was eventually made to recede by the appearance of a new active relationship in the child's mind: one to God in Heaven. Her celestial father replaced her earthly one, and the stability of her world became resurrected. Her visible behavior became strangely incomprehensible to those around her, but inwardly she was finding her way. I worked with this child for 2 or 3 years, and she became less reliant on God and seemed to be doing well. Twenty years later she earned a doctorate in theology, which I thought was interesting. Why should she not devote her life to the one who saved her sanity?

Madness in this case did not lie in the symptoms that were shown. The so-called symptoms in fact were the sanity returning to her world, or trying to. People who have stumbled into the abyss do all kinds of things to bring stability and substantiality back to their worlds, and it is a tragedy of our field that these efforts are confused and conflated with the madness itself. This is also seen in the case of the young woman who said that children were living in her bedroom. Those children, I suggested, may well have symbolized what remained of her psychological health.

One of the greatest challenges presented to those who have fallen into the abyss is the pervasive view in psychiatry that there is a disease process taking place within them. What a person in the grip of annihilation needs, above all else, is someone's understanding of the horror, which will include a human response assisting in the journey back to some sort of psychological survival. A person undergoing an experience of the total meltdown of the universe, when told that his or her suffering stems from a mental illness, will generally feel confused, invalidated, and undermined. Because there are no resources to fight against such a view, its power will have a petrifying effect on subjectivity and deepen the fall into the abyss.

An objectified psychiatric diagnosis is the antithesis of needed validation and mirroring. It leaves one with an attribution, offered up by a person invested with enormous authority, that can invade and usurp a person's sense of selfhood, that can operate like a nuclear-tipped torpedo exploding in one's brain. Imagine the situation of a young man in the midst of a fall into the abyss, who has the misfortune to become incarcerated in an institution typical of the ones we have today in America. Perhaps the patient's doctor, directly or indirectly, communicates the view that he is suffering from the brain *disease* known as schizophrenia. The annihilating impact of such a view then becomes symbolized in the patient's unfolding experience that vicious, destructive voices are speaking to him over invisible wires and saying repeatedly that he should die. In this way a spiraling effect occurs, wherein the operation of the medical model further injures the already devastated patient, whose reactions to the new injuries in turn reconfirm the correctness of the diagnosis. Around and around we go, and this is generally the situation of madness in America.

Is it not diagnosis, though, to identify someone as having fallen into the abyss, which is what I have said madness is? The words are different, but here too, don't we have a classification and a locating of the patient as a member of that particular class? To note that the particular experiences someone is having involve a fall into nonbeing involves a distinguishing and a knowing, and to that extent, etymologically speaking, one could say it is a diagnosis. But the word *diagnosis* has been absorbed into an objectifying, medical-language game, interlocking with all manner of terms and concepts about disease processes, biological roots, and treatment possibilities. So I would not want to use the term to describe one's apprehension that someone has fallen out of the world. Also, my response will be a very different one based on this apprehension—certainly I am not going to tell the patient he is a schizophrenic. I am also not going to say that she is mad.

The reason has to do with how such a thing will likely be heard—what terms like *schizophrenia* or even *madness* would mean to someone in an annihilation state. What I would want to do is communicate that I was listening, that I was understanding at least some part of what was being told to me, and that I was prepared to do whatever would be necessary to be of help. I would also always try to express all of this in a language that would be understood in the spirit I intended.

Imagine a patient who comes, speaking of his or her complete personal destruction. How might one respond to such an individual? It will depend on precisely what is said and how it is said as well as on my understanding of the unique situation of this particular person at this particular moment. There are no general formulas here, but I could give an example or two. Suppose a young woman tells me, as someone once did, that she is having hallucinatory visions of a most terrifying kind. She reports being swept away, through space, then physically shrinking and being drawn into the bloodstream of her mother's body. She is then tumbling helplessly within the coursing blood, trying not to drown, and her face and finally her whole body begin flaking away and dissolving. The vision culminates in a terrifying sense of disappearing altogether, having become indistinguishable from the blood. Again and again this vision came to her, sometimes it being other family members' bloodstreams into which she dissolved. She cried when she told me of these experiences, and begged me to tell her what was happening.

I did not tell her she was schizophrenic. I did not tell her she was mad. Such things had already been said to her by her psychoanalyst, a gentleman she had been seeing three times each week for the previous 8 years. When she complained to him about the hallucinatory immersions in her family's blood, he had responded by saying: "You are experiencing a series of transitory psychotic episodes, most likely brought on by serious stress." In essence her analyst was telling her she was crazy, and his reaction, unsurprisingly, was of no help. Unable to discern the core of subjective truth that was present in the strange experiences the patient was reporting, he focused instead on the ways in which her perception of what was happening to her departed from his definitions of objective reality.

In contrast, I let her telling and retelling of the frightening visions flow over my mind like a waterfall. A thought then came into my consciousness, which I decided to speak—for better or for worse. I said to the patient, calling her by her first name: "Marie, is it possible that your whole family is nothing but a bunch of bloodsucking vampires?" She was silent for 10 or 20 seconds, and then said that no one had ever said anything like that to her before. This was the first conversation I had with this patient, the first of a great, great many. The hallucinations vanished, never to return.

The story of her life then began to emerge. It was a story of extreme trauma and enmeshment, and she needed a long time to tell it fully. This process was not easy; it was arduous, requiring many years.

The hallucinations vanished because the metaphor they contained had been understood and validated, because there was a new relationship to someone with whom the truth could be spoken. She did come from a family of vampires. The analyst she had been seeing was himself also a vampire. But she had never known this as anything that was real to her—in fact, the appearance of the hallucination could be considered a spontaneous and quite profound improvement in her situation, because it contained a reality never before seen. Of course, she needed someone to understand what was being expressed; otherwise it would just have been something strange interfering with her functioning. Had it continued to be labeled and treated as a symptom of psychosis, I would imagine her situation would have grown even worse. I don't know if hallucinations in general can be handled so readily, but I do know that they often contain symbolic metaphors, sometimes expressing the very heart of the matter of what has gone awry in a person's life. It is obvious that our patients will do better if someone is available to understand these things than if there is not.

Another case that comes to mind in a similar connection is that of Daniel Paul Schreber (1911/2000), the German jurist whose *Memoirs of My Nervous Illness* were analyzed famously by Sigmund Freud (1911). Schreber said, to put it in its simplest terms, that he was the victim of a vast and deadly persecution, organized against him by God with the collusion of his own psychiatrist. His writings about this are highly elaborated, almost elegant equivalents to my patient's report of her hallucination of being dissolved into the bloodstreams of her relatives.

Let me imagine what one might have done with Schreber, and how he then might have responded himself. Of course the first thing would be to really try to hear what he was saying, and I mean *all* that he was saying, at every level of its meaning. I would listen to him as he told me of the *conspiracy* that had been directed against him. I would listen closely as he spoke of the horrifying *unmanning* to which he was being subjected by his psychiatrist and God, the final goal of which was to transform him body and soul into a *woman* and bring the process of *soul murder* to its terrible conclusion. I would listen attentively to his descriptions of the *divine rays* coming down from heaven and playing on his mind and body, and of the diabolical *miracles* taking place within him as a result of this supernatural activity. I would focus on his descriptions of the people surrounding him in the asylum as *fleeting improvised men*, simulacra apparently existing only for his benefit.

Not only would I sit with him as he spoke and carefully read over the manuscripts on which he worked; I would want to hear what he was saying and perhaps give him a sense of being listened to that he had never encountered before. Schreber may well have been a man that no one had ever listened to, at least not at the level of the deepest core of what he experienced. People in our field need to think about what it is like never to have been listened to—to have been raised in an empathic vacuum, or worse, a setting that closes out all that one might authentically feel and then authors and re-authors one's experience according to the design of alien agendas. This would include a family life that lays down layer upon layer of disqualification and invalidation, all the while insisting on total compliance. I see this man's background in such terms.

How does one accomplish such a level of listening? As in the case of the patient who was swept into her relatives' bloodstreams, I would let what is said flow over me like a waterfall and see what images and understandings begin to emerge. I picture listening to Schreber (1911/2000) tell of God deforming and transforming his body, of the miracles and the rays, of the soul murder being carried out. I would try not to hear any of this as delusion; nor, if there were voices speaking to him, would I think of them as hallucinations. The concepts of delusion and hallucination arise because we are hypnotized by what we think of as the externally real, and once the fascination sets in, we cannot hear what is said to us without judging its degree of concordance with that external reality. It is possible, though, to set such thoughts aside and listen to what is being said, in and for itself.

In Daniel Paul Schreber (1911/2000), I see a child locked in a power struggle with a parent—there is evidence that it was his father (Schatzman, 1973; Orange, 1995)—a struggle for existence itself. The ideas of unmanning and being made into a woman involve a stripping away of what makes this male child who he is. It converts him from someone who has a right to his own existence—who is in possession of his own masculine power to act and think—into a woman, which in this historical context probably means a passive vessel of pure receptivity and cooperativeness. This is another way of picturing the fall into the abyss, the erasure of one's very soul. The child—to whom all of this has happened and is happening—is telling his story in the so-called delusions and hallucinations, and if that story is heard, that might make all the difference for Schreber. I would want to let him know that I was listening, and that he was succeeding in making me hear what he was trying to say. I would also want to emphasize how I saw that his *Memoirs* constitute a kind of resurrection of his soul, a reclaiming of the life that had been stolen away from him.

Regarding the "fleeting improvised men" Schreber said he witnessed around him, the following thoughts come to mind. If other people in Schreber's world are construed as a swirling of temporarily assembled appearances, then others are reduced to arbitrary beings having no real substance of their own. This amounts to the ultimate triumph of the will: The whole human world becomes subject to Schreber's subjectivity; in a way, he becomes the only being who is real—an epistemological tyrant with absolute power over the very existence of all other beings. This is a reversal of his original predicament, in which Schreber the child is fashioned into a contraption that materializes his father's fantasy of the perfect child. So the original improvised man was none other than Daniel Paul Schreber.

I think of a contrast here. Another patient on whose treatment I consulted some years ago believed that she had been kidnapped into the movie, *The Truman Show* (i.e., that her every act and even her every thought was being broadcast across our country for the entertainment of the population). Her life had thus become a television show, and she had been stripped of her own autonomy and personal subjectivity. Here we have the sovereign power of the Other, in whose gaze the whole of one's being has become absorbed. She had come to feel that she resided exclusively in the mass perception of the American people. Schreber is the reverse: He thought that the masses of people resided solely in his own perception; that they were little more than figments of his imagination, transitory little entities assembled to entertain or otherwise preoccupy him. And yet, still and all, Schreber was himself, in the beginning, a fleeting improvised child.

Working in the territory of annihilated souls is never easy. To really listen to someone, anyone, to hear the depth of what he or she may have felt, to work one's way into realms of experience perhaps never before perceived by anyone and therefore never articulated—all of this is as hard a task as one may undertake. Maybe I would try to listen to Schreber and tell him I was doing so by sitting with him day after day, month after month, year after year if need be. I know I would never tell him that he was mentally ill. I certainly would not inform him of his diagnosis of dementia praecox or schizophrenia. Those communications could only deepen his fall into the abyss. I am quite sure his psychiatrist, someone he considered his mortal enemy, spoke to him in precisely such a way and contributed greatly to his destruction. I might even tell Schreber that he was among the sanest people I had ever met, because I knew he was a man who spoke the truth.

It is possible that Schreber would be able to see in my eyes and on my face the recognition and acknowledgment he was seeking, and that nothing more would be needed. Often the simple presence of another human being who is actually listening to the story that is being told is all that is required. Schreber was utterly brilliant, with a sensitive understanding of other people and a penetrating intellect. If someone were really paying attention, it would not be lost upon him.

THE HUMAN CAUSES OF MADNESS

If we approach madness as a human experience, then we would seek knowledge of what causes it in human terms. I had a colleague once who came to me and said he agreed with my thinking about this, explaining that he had discovered that people actually "choose" madness, or at least that it arises out of the decisions they make in the exercise of their freedom. I found I had to disagree with this individual. No one "chooses" madness, and no one "chooses" something that leads to madness. In fact, the abyss includes the dissolution of choice itself, as all basis in self-experience for agentic action of any kind vanishes absolutely.

What then are the circumstances under which madness occurs? I already gave a partial answer to this by referring to the idea of a failure of the sustaining matrix of relationships to others that our sanity is based upon. This is not an environmentalism casting the person as passive victim. A failure in the sustaining ties that one has to others is not external or environmental, and it is not internal or mental. We need to escape these snares of dualism. It is something that happens subjectively—something felt, lived, and endured by the person in whose life the madness erupts. That is the beginning, the middle, and the end. It arises out of the utterly disastrous situational contexts in which we find ourselves. Obviously we have a role in creating our situations, favorable or unfavorable. But thinking about the origin of madness requires a different mindset altogether, one that highlights the specific sequence of events occurring in the subjective field of the person's experience.

Let me offer another example. Picture a young man, a brilliant physicist and mathematician, someone whose thinking was beyond the minds of his contemporaries in most respects. Imagine further that this man never learned how to relate closely and sensitively with other people, in part because of his exceptional scientific talents and preoccupying interests. He remained, nevertheless, very vulnerable to others' reactions and opinions, and felt searing shame and humiliation when his socially awkward ways led others to think he was strange and to withdraw from him. In the extreme, if someone treated him with hostility and contempt, he actually began to fragment, and avoided such terrible experiences by keeping almost entirely to himself.

Now picture this man, still in his youth but already working at a high level as a physicist, availing himself of the one experience that shored up his otherwise frequently crumbling selfhood: exposing himself to other young men in a public urinal. Here he was, a brilliant scientist, letting it all hang out in the restroom of a public park. Envision the police arriving in a sting operation, arresting him for indecency, and then communicating with his employer and colleagues about the crime he had been caught committing. Disaster upon disaster, catastrophe on catastrophe: Soon he was fired from his position at a prestigious science institute because of what was seen as unforgivable, intolerable moral depravity.

The story is not over. Our friend, the incomparable mathematician/physicist, experienced all this as the worst attack on his personal selfhood that had ever occurred: one that defined him, seemingly irrevocably, as a sex pervert. An explosion took place in the center of his being, one in which all sense of coherent, cohesive identity was blown to pieces, and all that was left was a need for unification. Time passed. Terrible, unspeakable agonies occurred. Then, as if brought to him by a magical cloud, an idea appeared that promised to solve everything. His destiny was to achieve the unified field theory—that structure of mathematical and physical concepts that will finally bring Einstein's theory of relativity together with the theory of quantum mechanics. Over the next period, he poured himself into the search for the equations that would help the macroscopic universe make contact with microscopic phenomena in the quantum domain, a theory that will disclose the previously hidden variables that can unify gravity with the electromagnetic and other forces of nature. Anticipating glory, he celebrated in imagination the lecture he would give upon receiving the Nobel Prize. Thereby, in fantasy, he pulled the fragments together, displaying a shining coherence for all the world to see. The humiliated, devastated, annihilated soul thus moved toward its own redemption.

One minor difficulty: The scientific problem he had set out to solve is just too hard. Even though he was brilliant, unifying the foundations of physics required something he was unable to provide, no matter how hard he tried. Working late into the night—night after night, month after month—nothing came forward to bring the division together despite writing innumerable pages of equations, and his efforts continued to accelerate in the face of frustration and failure.

A vision finally supervened in the midst of this desperate activity: The world itself had become fractured and fragmented into isolated, often warring nations. Our friend now saw his future in even more glorious terms: to bring together the world itself, to heal the divisions that have torn it apart, to establish a unifying world government and usher in everlasting human peace. In this quest he appointed himself Emperor of the Earth, whose sovereign rule would establish a human utopia. Guiding messages and confirmations of his destiny were received, telepathically, from advanced civilizations in other galaxies. At this point he actually traveled to various foreign capitals and tried to establish contact with the governing authorities so that his unifying dream could be fulfilled. His behavior, now having become disruptive of the routines of ordinary life, drew the attention of neighbors. The police were called, and he was incarcerated in a psychiatric asylum. A very sad story.

He was trying to put the shattered world back together, but the human environment was not supporting his efforts on behalf of unification; it was instead attacking him, imprisoning him, and declaring him crazy. No man is an island, and so an intergalactic Thou crystallized an Other to support and sustain his efforts to reintegrate and climb back out of the abyss. Here again, we see how the struggle to regain one's footing, to reestablish one's very being, is perceived as an illness by everyone within that person's social orbit.

Our friend was subjected to psychiatric violence, including involuntary incarceration, intrusive and powerful medications, and insulin and electroshock therapy. He was also told that he was mentally ill—specifically, that he was a schizophrenic. This did not help, in that it repeated and exacerbated the other things that had occurred to make him feel terrible about himself. The so-called treatment added to the fragmentation and deepened the fall into the abyss.

Finally, drawing on resources no one knew were available to him, he took matters into his own hands. Ceasing to speak of his mission to unify the planet and the inspiring messages from space, he focused his efforts on giving his doctors what they wanted to see: a man who was oriented to his surroundings, in contact with the externally real, and intent on resuming a normal life. He was still getting his messages and inwardly had not given up on destiny, but he was teaching himself not to speak about it, and not even to think about it all very much. His doctors, in turn, stopped telling him he was crazy, and former colleagues began to express interest in him again. Finally, he was pronounced dramatically improved and released from his long captivity. He subsequently worked on the periphery of his former field, and I understand he did well for many years.

Madness comes about as a result of the failure of sustaining human relationships. It arises out of disastrous trauma that challenges the person's very capacity to experience "I am." Sometimes the precipitating events are present, clear, and dramatic; at other times, the inner catastrophes are hidden, perhaps lost in the mists of very early life. Whatever the details of the particular genesis, madness is a human response in a human context.

3

Philosophy and Psychotherapy

When my mother died I was very young,
And my father sold me while yet my tongue
Could scarcely cry.

William Blake

I recently listened to a lecture in which the speaker said that every psychotherapist must be a philosopher. I think of philosophy as that domain of thought that brings us to an awareness of our deepest assumptions, and certainly psychotherapists should in this sense become philosophers. But in my old age, I find that I have become impatient with discussions that become too abstract. So I shall address this topic with a series of clinical stories, ones that to some extent relate to major areas of philosophy: metaphysics, the nature of the real; ethics, the nature of the good; epistemology, the nature of knowing; and aesthetics, the nature of the beautiful.

METAPHYSICS: THE NATURE OF THE REAL

My first story concerns a 30-year-old man with whom I sat down a long time ago when I was still a student, a man who had been given a diagnosis of schizophrenia. He was silent, for a number of minutes.

I asked him finally: "What are you thinking about, brother?" The answer that came back was: "I don't think. It thinks." When I asked him what "it" was, he answered: "The machine. It is. I am not."

No matter what I said after this initial interchange, he kept repeating the statement that he did not think, was not there, and there was only a machine. What does one make of such statements? Most people would regard his words as in plain contradiction to all that is real. That would also be the view of contemporary psychiatry.

My encounter with this gentleman took place during my student days, at a time when I had not yet understood the phenomenology of annihilation states and the imagery often used to express and symbolize it. Instead I was still captive to a Cartesian view, in which this patient seemed to have traveled into an alternate universe, a world of his own that had lost contact with objective reality. Phenomenological contextualism had not yet been born. How, I wondered, is one to establish communication with such a person? Conversation between human beings, I thought, requires a shared basis of understanding, and here we had a rift separating his world from ours. What is one supposed to do with such a discrepancy? Do we suspend our own reality and try to enter his? Do we tell him he is wrong and try to draw him into ours?

There was no real guidance in the psychiatric setting where this was occurring, and neither I nor the other students and clinicians available were able to do anything constructive with this patient. He was eventually transferred to a long-term care facility for the chronically mentally ill. But I have never forgotten him, and I have tried to rethink what I experienced then in the light of my later training and clinical adventures.

I would now relate what this man said to the way I had initially addressed him. The question asking him what he was thinking about might have implied to him that there was a "he" or a "you" within him capable of being spoken to. If there is no such being, the posing of the question opens up a gulf of misunderstanding and invalidation that might well have ended the communication even before it had begun. People carrying the diagnosis of schizophrenia often do not experience themselves as existing. They live in a felt state of nonbeing. As a result, the customary ways of being addressed in our society cast them into a nowhere zone: unseen, unacknowledged. They then react to this banishment, and their reactions to the misunderstanding, in turn, are viewed as symptoms of the illness from which they are said to suffer. This is the situation of madness in America.

When I asked him about himself, and then persisted even when he had told me he was not there, I committed an act of infinite abandonment and invalidation. It would have been far better if I had simply sat by his side, quietly, knowing that he felt my presence.

Furthermore, when I addressed him as "brother," I made an attribution he cannot possibly have been able to make sense of. I was not his brother. He was no one's brother, in that he was no one at all. To be construed as such was to be swept into a controlling agenda that was unrelated to the nonbeing that was his authentic state. So the machine arrived: something that spoke, that had thoughts, that perceived. I, George Atwood, may well have been that machine, annihilating what little remained of his personhood by misguided friendliness. As the man told me, he was not—there was only the machine. Looking back now, I find that I like this man, because he spoke the truth as he saw it. There was hope for such a gentleman, but I was certainly of no help at the time.

People in annihilation states are not for that reason inaccessible to communication. One could have focused on the purely physical and directed the conversation to the way the patient was dressed, or to the heat or the oppressive humidity. One could have spoken to him in the third person—individuals in the midst of nonbeing do not experience "I am," and often therefore cannot tolerate being addressed as "you." It might have been a good idea to bring him a cup of coffee and doughnuts and talk to him about how good or bad they tasted. One could rest there quietly or take him for a walk.

This patient was someone living in a state of utter catastrophe, but opportunities were there to be with him without making his situation worse. If one ascribed something to him he was not able to experience, however, he was catapulted into the grip of the machine.

In approaching this man, it would have been good to start with the unremarkable idea that he, and I, and everyone all live in a common world. Perhaps this is a philosophical assumption, but I don't see how one could speak to anyone about anything on any other basis. One would have needed not to overstress his talk about the machine and his absence—he was experiencing these things, but they do not mean he lived in an alternate universe. They were just particular points at which his subjective life did not correspond to mine; there were plenty of other points at which there was no significant disparity.

If I wanted to relate to him, a space had to be created in which he could begin to feel himself in my presence and myself in his. A firm handshake and a squeeze on the shoulder might have begun to establish this, and then could be followed up by a comment or two directed to our shared physical situation. Perhaps he would have said nothing in response, but he might have been listening.

I could have brought out the coffee and doughnuts and offered them to him. I might have warned him that the coffee was very hot and asked if he wanted any milk or sugar in it. If he still did not respond, I could pour coffee for myself and bite into a doughnut, then telling him how good or how bad it tasted. Who knows? A foundation might have been laid for a healing relationship with him.

What is it that might have happened though in this man's life? How do people come to an experience of not being there, and of there only being a machine? Those who feel they are not present, and who affirm the existence of a machine that controls their minds and bodies, are often the products of profound enmeshment with their caregivers in childhood. An accommodation has taken place at a very young age in which the agenda of the caregiver—it can be the mother, the father, or both—becomes the supreme principle defining the child's developing sense of personal identity. The experience of the child as an independent person in his or her own right is nullified, so that the child the parents wish for can be brought into being. Very often there are no outward signs of anything amiss, as family life unfolds in a seeming harmony. Somewhere along the way, however, the false self begins to crumble, and a sense of the degree to which the child has been absent from life arises. This emerging feeling of having never been there, of having been controlled and regulated by outside forces, is so unstable and fragmentary that it is given concrete form. What is seen from the viewpoint of others as a delusion then begins to crystallize, for example in the image of an influencing machine (Tausk, 1917; Orange et al., 1997, chap. 4). Within the world of the child, now perhaps chronologically an adult, the so-called delusion is a carrier of a truth that has up until then been entirely hidden and erased. What looks like a breakdown into psychosis and delusion thus may represent an attempted breakthrough, but the inchoate "I" does require an understanding and responsive "Thou" in order to have a chance to consolidate itself. This could well be the situation of the patient described in my little story, and the challenge to be faced by anyone who might have chosen to continue with him. It would unquestionably have been a very long journey.

In another case, I was walking with a young woman, a 24-year-old, on the grounds of a psychiatric hospital where she had been for a number of months. Like the last case, she had been diagnosed as schizophrenic. There was silence as we began our walk, but then she turned to me and said the following:

> You know, George, there is a cavern beneath this hospital, and there are assassins that hide in it. At night they come out and murder the patients. I think they work for the CIA. Every hospital in America has a cavern.

I did not know how to respond. I think I just said, "Wow!" She stared into my eyes for 5 or 10 seconds, and then shouted a series of questions and demanded answers:

> Do you believe what I just told you? Tell me if you think it is true: Is there a cavern, or is it just that I am mentally ill? Am I right

about this, or am I sick? Which is it? Tell me right now, you bastard! Do you believe? I want to know: True, or Sick? Yes, or No?

I knew better than to tell this patient she was mentally ill, but I could not bring myself to say that I believed her. We struggled for a few minutes with this, and finally I tore myself away and left, with her screaming at me. It seemed that I was damned if I did and damned if I didn't. If I told her she was mentally ill, she would feel condemned and invalidated. If I said I believed her, she would see I was lying. That might be worse than saying she was crazy. Also, I could almost hear my psychiatrist colleagues telling me that believing the delusion would be a matter of encouraging psychotic thinking.

This story traces back about 30 years, at a time that my ideas about annihilation states and their connection to experiences of invalidation were first crystallizing. I happened at the time to pick up a paper written by one of my own former students, a clinician who was employed at a large public mental health center. She had worked for years as an outpatient psychotherapist, often with young men and women who were very seriously emotionally disturbed. The overall philosophy of this psychiatric institution was based on the medical model, and its primary mode of treatment was the provision of psychiatric drugs. My student had grown more and more appalled over the period of her employment by what she thought was damaging mistreatment and unforgivable neglect. I looked at the title of her paper, and it seemed to cry out to me: "Contemporary treatment of young adults in community mental health centers: Are we murdering a generation of geniuses?"

My patient had been claiming murders were taking place in her hospital, and at all the psychiatric hospitals in our country. It occurred to me that she and my student were talking about the same thing. It was a symbolic metaphor, containing a deep subjective truth. I asked myself also why my patient was describing the assassins in the cavern as coming out only at night. She was saying they do their deadly work secretly, out of anyone's sight. The medically oriented treatment of her institution presented itself as a constructive, healing procedure. In the daylight world, it therefore manifested in a form that one would hope would be of help to those receiving it. But its invalidating, discrediting impact was hidden, and took its toll on the souls of the so-called mentally ill out of public view. In other words, it occurred in the dark.

The patient had been told repeatedly that she was a schizophrenic. I began to think about what it feels like to be seen in this way—to have anything and everything one does viewed as a symptom of the most severe mental illness that exists. One needs to imagine this experience, and take into consideration that the person being so viewed is also someone in the midst of personal disaster already. We have a human being for whom the bottom has completely fallen out, who struggles to maintain the most basic sense of integrity, perhaps even of existence itself. Then that individual becomes subject to an unrelenting experience of being personally discredited and pathologized. Psychiatric hospitals, which should be healing asylums, by and large are annihilation factories instead. The murders that are committed there are soul murders, and the medical model itself is one of the primary instrumentalities of this infernal work. If one tells the patient she is mentally ill, one completes the killing.

Listening to my patient's words softly—symbolically and metaphorically—they convey a message about the emotional violence happening to her as a result of psychiatric objectification. I began to see that what she was saying was, from her viewpoint, completely true. I also discovered something else that gave me pause: Many psychiatric hospitals do have tunnels beneath the floors on which the patients are housed. These tunnels are often used for unobtrusively removing the bodies of those who have died or committed suicide. All of this helped me find a way to respond to the young woman that did not make the situation worse.

I decided, based on these reflections, that my patient was right, that there was indeed a cavern of assassins beneath the hospital, and that murders were indeed taking place each and every night. So I decided to tell her just that. The next time we met, she was waiting for me with those same urgent questions, repeated over and over. I asked her to listen to my response:

> My dear, listen to me. I have to apologize for running out on you the last time I was here and not answering your questions. The problem was that I did not understand what you were asking me, although you were being very clear. Now I do understand and I am going to tell you what I think. You are speaking the truth. Death is everywhere at this hospital, and you are also right that it is present at every hospital in our country. This is not illness; this is you speaking the plain, unvarnished truth. My answer to you is Yes, Yes, Yes!

She was satisfied, and the imagery of the cavern and the assassins receded. I never heard another word about it in the long and continuing course of my relationship with her. The incident I have been describing occurred very early in our work together, only a few months after I first met her. But there were signs that something very good had happened in the subsequent period. Perhaps a week after the discussions about caverns and murders had come to an end, I was walking with her again over the hospital grounds. I never knew what to say to this patient, so I would just say anything that came to my mind. On this day, I asked her: "Tell me. What is the most beautiful thing you have seen today, on this lovely morning we are sharing?" She answered with the following words: "I saw a beautiful flower growing at the center of a cold, gray rock."

I had understood already that the patient had been subject to feelings of inner deadness for a number of years. She had cut herself really seriously 2 months earlier—deep slashes across her chest and on her arms performed with a coffee can lid. I had originally thought she was trying to commit suicide in this terrible act; but she informed me that she had wanted to feel the intensity of the pain and see her bright red blood flow. She had been in an experience of numbness and deadness and, rather than intending to die, was desperately seeking signs and sensations of life.

So I thought the rock might be a symbol of that deadness, an enclosing prison in which there were no feelings and there was no life. But she was telling me now that life had appeared in the midst of death, and that it was a beautiful flower. This had to be a good sign for her and for our connection. I did not put my thoughts into any direct words, but chose instead to suggest that she and I compose a poem about that lovely flower. We sat on the edge of a pond in the morning sunlight and wrote one out, which she chose to entitle "The Midnight Blue Rose." The patient did well in the ensuing years and was eventually able to leave the hospital and live with family members. Our work continued for many decades.

Not all such cases end on a positive note, however. A well-established psychiatrist of my acquaintance was recently murdered by a young man who came to his office late at night. The patient was in a panic because he believed he was being poisoned in a vast conspiracy. He begged the doctor to help him find a way to rid his body of the toxins that had accumulated, crying out that this was his last chance to survive. The persecutors, as the man described them, were led by a number of psychiatrists and other mental health professionals, in league with various relatives who had turned against him. There was also some talk about a strange machine that was involved with his suffering.

The doctor, himself a respected but very conventional person working in Manhattan, made a diagnosis of paranoid schizophrenia, and gently but firmly advised the patient to begin on a course of antipsychotic medications he would prescribe. The patient listened to this advice, and pulled out a knife and plunged it into the doctor's heart. I know what happened because I was able to look at interview material collected from the patient by the police shortly after the murder.

So here we have someone again living in what looks like a different reality, and in this case the effort to connect with him precipitated lethal violence. A clash of worlds occurred here, ending in homicide. The psychiatrist in this awful story "knew" his patient was delusional, and he "knew" the so-called delusion was a symptom of a mental illness that could only be treated with medications. I have a series of thoughts about the calamitous situation that then developed.

Let us start with the antipsychotic medications. These drugs are actually poisonous, and I wonder about the patient's complaints being the result of negative physiological reactions to their presence in his body. He claimed toxins had accumulated within him, and the chemicals likely to be involved here are known to be toxic. But the doctor responded not by addressing the possible validity of the patient's complaints, but instead by prescribing more of what the young man said was poisoning him. This was a very bad decision on the psychiatrist's part, and it led to him being killed.

As in the earlier examples, there are points at which the patient's experience here departed substantially from all that this doctor believed to be real. The physician viewed his patient as engaging in paranoid distortions of efforts to help him on the part of other clinicians, for example, and it is likely he also saw the patient's relatives as equally to have been drawn into a paranoid delusional system. The patient, by contrast, was in the midst of an experience of being plotted against and attacked by a whole range of individuals, some of whom probably were the people to whom he originally turned for help. It strikes me as something of a miracle that there was still a particle of hope left inside this young man, as evidenced by his coming to my colleague in the middle of the night. What a sad and tragic thing it is that this court of last resort, as its first action, joined the conspiracy that was destroying the patient. A physician lies dead, and the young man is destined to spend the rest of his life incarcerated in mental institutions. It probably did not have to end this way.

What other way could have been found, and what other ending might have taken place? That leads to my second thought, concerning how the doctor might otherwise have responded, and what experience then the patient might have had in consequence. What if the first thing the doctor did was to ask about the specific poisons that had been introduced into his system by those that had hurt him so terribly? Let me imagine that the patient knew the names of the drugs that he had been given, and that they were the standard medications given by professionals in our field for psychosis.

I picture the possibility, not embraced obviously by the doomed psychiatrist, of having given the patient a specific, point-by-point summary of the destructive effects of his various medications. One could speak of the dangers of tardive dyskinesia, of diabetes, of various cardiac effects, of lasting alterations of the neurochemical environment within the brain, of excessive weight gain and its complications, of temporary and permanent interferences with cognitive functioning, of generalized emotional numbing that makes a person feel he or she has become a zombie.

I also imagine one could have instructed the patient about exactly what he needed to do in order to stop such effects and reduce any reliance there might have been on the tranquilizing action of the medications he had been taking. I might have said to him that if he wanted to detoxify his body and get away from these substances, he had come to the right place. I would promise him I would see that he received the help he needed and he would accomplish what he was trying to do. I seriously doubt a murder would have occurred, because what reason would there have been for it?

Someone like this is in a state of terror and despair. My goal would be to relieve him of the fear and provide a reason for hope on which he and I could build. The literal content of what I was suggesting is less important than the message of reassurance I would be trying to give to him. I would be speaking to him in a language that is the only one he was in a position to understand at this desperate moment of his destroyed life.

Maybe I should also say that if I had seen he had a knife, and suspected he might use it on me, I would have done everything in my power to physically escape the situation. I would have run out of the building and called the police. It is a cardinal principle of my practice never to allow myself to be killed, and there have actually been some close calls.

My third thought about this story, however, concerns what it meant in terms of the patient's probable life history. Here he was, feeling poisoned by persecutors, running to a man who was his last hope. The situation lends itself to an interpretation along the lines of the persecutors being symbols of maternal malevolence and the doctor being a rescuing paternal authority. This is a memory of a little boy who runs to his father after being massively threatened by something happening with his mother. He seems not to have received much help from his father though, because how otherwise would he have ended up in this condition? Still and all, the presence of hope remains in the picture, however tenuously; that is, it remains until it is destroyed by the psychiatrist's response. I would expect the patient to want to kill himself after murdering the doctor—the violence is a sign of his despair having become absolute and everlasting.

My final thoughts concern the possible course of events in this case if a better response to the patient had been given. I will draw on clinical experiences I have had in a situation not dissimilar to this one. I would imagine seeing this young man on a very frequent basis, probably every day in the initial weeks. I treated such a person many years ago, and we met every morning in a local diner for breakfast. I had no openings in my regular schedule, so this was the only basis on which we could have time together.

My patient was initially very fearful of meeting me in public, saying his enemies were everywhere and intended to kill him. I answered these fears with a simple declaration: "As long as you and I are meeting, your enemies will not hurt you. I guarantee it." This helped him begin to relax, but it was many days before he calmed down enough to join me in actually having breakfast. I did not wait, however, and so for the first week and a half he had to watch me consume cheese omelets, French toast, pancakes, hash browns, and fruit, even as he sat there eating and drinking nothing. It was kind of pathetic to look at this poor, hungry, frightened man while I was feasting. Eventually though he ordered some bacon and coffee, and things improved. A foundation was thereby created for a very long and productive relationship. This patient eventually weaned himself off the antipsychotic medications he had been taking and recovered essentially completely from a paranoia that had been present for many years.

So I would try to repeat this good experience by inviting the young man to breakfast over the ensuing period. I would certainly expect him to be suspicious, but I would disarm him by unrelenting friendliness, and I would order food for him in the hope that he might accept it. In the meantime, he could be tapering off the medications he thought were poisoning him, and, who knows, maybe he could get off them entirely over the course of a few weeks or months. In pursuing this strategy I would be building on the spark of hope I saw at work in his first contacting me.

Where has this discussion left us with respect to the topic I began with: the role of philosophy in psychotherapy with a focus on metaphysics? Certainly there is nothing that has emerged to help us define the nature of the ultimately real. Here are three assumptions, and one can call them philosophical: First, we live in a common world; second, people are experiencing beings; and third, not everyone sees things in the same way. Adhering to these ideas helps us discover ways to respond to many of the otherwise incomprehensible and obscure things presented in extreme psychological disturbances.

ETHICS: THE QUESTION OF THE GOOD

We are our brothers' and sisters' keepers. We are all siblings in the same darkness, as my friend Robert Stolorow likes to say. We are the guardians of the earth and all its living creatures. These are the tenets of my ethical philosophy, and in my professional work I have always tried to give it expression.

I can describe a case that appears to raise ethical issues and questions, and then discuss how my philosophical attitude plays out in a specific human context. The story involves a tragedy. This is the story of a suicidal patient, a woman of 49, who announced in a tone of certainty that she planned to end her life. It was only a question of when, not if. She showed an interest in the possibility of psychotherapy during the short period she would be remaining alive. She was without question going to kill herself, but considered it potentially beneficial to speak to someone nevertheless about her situation. No one was available to her, however, because all the clinicians she contacted said that they would work to avert her death. She had no interest in speaking to such a person.

What would I do if called upon by this woman? She insisted she was going to end her life, but asked for an opportunity for some counseling over the short period remaining to her. I have said we are our brothers' and sisters' keepers: How does this principle apply to someone who has elected to die?

Another feature of the situation was that she refused to speak to anyone who would form any sort of attachment to her. Above all, it was required that her therapist, if she could find one, be someone who would not be hurt by her suicide. The freedom to die without having to worry about her therapist's feelings was an absolute condition of her agreeing to undertake the counseling. So she was looking for someone to talk to who would neither interfere with her planned death nor be negatively affected by it when it occurred. This is obviously about something.

Two factors seem to have been involved in her decision: first, that she was the child of Holocaust survivors, and had in her childhood been made to feel the purpose of her existence was to honor the dead rather than live a life of her own; and second, that she had become massively addicted to a variety of drugs and alcohol, and saw no possibility of recovering from this. She said her life had zero meaning for her, was filled with suffering, and needed to end.

Why was it, though, that she was interested in some form of counseling before her death? She seemed to want to wrap things up in a conversation with someone, if she could find a person who would not obstruct her in carrying out her decision. She said only that she thought it might be useful. I think I see that this woman's life depended on the locating of that person. All that remained here of the will to live was her interest in a short period of so-called counseling. She wanted to talk about the meaning of her situation, and the life force resides inside such a desire. I would assume that if she could not locate anyone to provide this, she would carry out her suicide.

That is exactly what occurred: All the clinicians she contacted made it clear they wanted to help her recover a wish to live. These included two psychotherapists whom I, ill-advisedly, recommended. The therapists also responded in a way indicating to her that they would be very upset if she committed suicide and would regard their work with her to have been a failure. This was intolerable to her, so she skipped the counseling and killed herself. The method she chose showed her absolute determination: She overdosed on a lethal amount of sleeping medications, drank a whole fifth of vodka on top of that, and put a plastic bag over her head so that she would suffocate. She really meant business. A very sad part of this story is that I had finally decided I would undertake the task of her counseling myself, but when I called her, she was already gone.

A person falls into despair, the world destroys her last particle of hope, and she kills herself. This woman turned to the professionals in our field for help, and they turned away from her. Suicides occur when hope is destroyed, and my philosophy includes the idea we should support hope rather than extinguish it. I would not, however, regard this as involving any ethical failure on anyone's part; the problem was their human failure, due to emotional stupidity. They knew not what they were doing.

I have said that I try to live by the principle that we are our brothers' and sisters' keepers, and yet this woman wanted a carte

blanche on ending her life as a condition for even entering psychotherapy. How could one have reconciled the one aspect of this and
the other? I would ask: Why was it that she needed her therapist,
if she could have found one, to be someone who would not oppose
her suicide and be negatively affected by it? It is obvious from the
brief story, as I think about it. There was no basis for continuing
to struggle and suffer, since she had been slated for a life of honor-
ing the already dead. Her parents harnessed her very being into
their everlasting trauma and grief, and within this project there
was no room for her existence as a person in her own right. She
was one of those whose life was never her own. Such people often
kill themselves.

I would have seen her life, what little there was of it, inhabiting
her wish to find someone who would not be hurt by her suicide.
This is, evidently, all that was left of this woman, and I would have
wanted to communicate that I understood what she was doing
and she was not to concern herself with protecting my feelings. In
the meantime, perhaps we could have had some good conversations. If she felt free in my presence not to take care of me, and at
liberty as well to end her life at any moment of her choosing, it is
possible that a space would have opened up she had never known
before, a space that belonged entirely to her. Who knows what
could have happened then? If I had not been too late, a miracle
might have occurred.

The ostensible care and concern of the clinicians she sought
out precipitated her suicide, and what I have proposed would have
been a chance for her survival. If we open our hearts and minds,
a pathway might then be found to our brothers and sisters that
otherwise would be lost to us.

This death might well have been inevitable, but at least she
would have had the opportunity to talk her story over with someone before signing off. Even then I would have known I had been
my sister's keeper, or done everything I could based on my understanding of her, and I could have lived with her death. I wonder
how the clinicians who told her they wanted to preserve her life

feel about it now. If I were one of them, I would be suffering very significantly.

EPISTEMOLOGY: THE DARKNESS OF UNKNOWING

The focus on philosophical themes seems to create opportunities for interesting discussions, so I shall continue by shifting to another domain of philosophy, that of epistemology. I have tried to think of clinical cases for which considerations bearing on the theory of knowledge would be germane. Epistemology asks such questions as: What is knowledge and what are its preconditions? The term *epistemological trauma* arises.

An epistemological trauma is an event that undercuts someone's faith in what previously had been believed to be true. It is an event or situation in a person's life that contradicts what had theretofore been a matter of the given or even pregiven. The effect of such a trauma is the shattering of confidence in one's own mind. Such a collapse of trust in oneself can lead to terrible things, even, in the extreme, to an experience of personal annihilation. It makes a person feel he or she has been cast into the darkness of unknowing, and nothing can make it better.

Two clinical stories come to mind, both involving patients of mine from many years ago. These are the people who introduced me to the concept of epistemological trauma. The first one involves a woman, 50 years old, who had been married for 24 years and in that period raised two sons. She came to me in a state of consuming anxiety, weeping uncontrollably, unable to sleep, desperate for help. Her marriage had not been perfect, but she and her husband had gotten along well enough and had cooperated for the most part in helping with the care of the sons. Their life together had been outwardly a conventional one—they belonged to a church, participated in community activities, had a number of friends they met during their children's school years.

Here is what happened: It suddenly emerged that for the entirety of their marriage the husband had maintained a secret homosexual life, one replete with sadomasochism, innumerable one-night stands, and, in the early years, incidents of prostituting himself for rich businessmen visiting his area. He suddenly told his wife he had filed for divorce and wanted to explore the life that up until then had been kept secret. This was presented in a mood of joyful exuberance, as he felt he had finally broken out of a prison of secrecy to a glorious freedom he had never known. He gave his wife a detailed, X-rated account of all the activities he formerly had felt it necessary to conceal and asked her to join in the celebration of his joy.

She passed into unconsciousness in the face of her husband's revelations, unable even to understand what he was trying to tell her. It later seemed he had changed into someone she did not recognize, and she struggled with the thought that he had been kidnapped and brainwashed into the ideas he was expressing. Then the bottom began to fall out, as she spiraled into a deep well of unknowing, losing faith in her ability to work, to relate adequately to her children and friends, to cook, even to choose her clothing in the morning when she got dressed. She told me in our first meeting that she felt she had lost her mind and was insane. She said as well that she had been mentally ill all her life and that terrible things must have happened to her when she was a young child to cause her deep emotional problems. I also met her two sons, and they were exhausted from trying to deal with their mother's distress and asked for her to be hospitalized.

I did not hospitalize her—it seemed clear to me that this would have made the situation worse and would have totally failed to address the trauma that precipitated her struggles. She needed something to arrest the spiral of unknowing and reverse the associated collapse in her self-esteem. I spoke to her for an hour and a half about her marriage, her life, and her suffering, and at the end of that time she had recovered her balance.

This dramatic effect arose out of the following: After listening to her, I simply told her what I thought was going on. There is nothing more powerful than human understanding. I told her she was not insane, that her life did not show any mental illness at all, and that she should just forget about such ideas. I added that there was some madness in the picture to be sure, her husband's. It seemed apparent from the story that he had entered a prolonged manic episode, and that this had caused him to turn his life, and his family's lives, upside down.

I explained she was in shock because everything she had believed had suddenly been upended, and this had made her lose faith in her own perceptions and feelings. I added that her reaction was normal in view of what had happened, and I explained that she would recover her balance as the traumatic shock gradually wore off. In the grip of her crisis, believing she had experienced a complete nervous breakdown, she had earlier requested antipsychotic and antidepressant medications. I told her she did not need anything like that, because she showed no trace of psychosis and no depressive illness either. I suggested that if the anxiety continued and interfered with her sleeping, she could take a small dose of Xanax before going to bed.

As I spoke in this way to my patient, and I had to repeat myself several times, she stared at me, blinking, at first not seeming to hear what I was saying. But then I saw my words were sinking in, and her relaxation was visible. She stopped fidgeting and looking around fearfully, and a deep calm seemed then to slowly materialize.

I know that it may be difficult to believe a simple conversation like this would permanently relieve this patient's confusion and suffering. I had to see her again a few times over the ensuing months and years, because the epistemological trauma continued to undermine the decisions she was making in reconstructing a life for herself after her husband's departure. For example, a year and a half later, she fell in love with a very kind gentleman, but she was terrified this move was setting the stage for a repetition of the disaster that had occurred in her marriage. She needed me to help her see that the doubt she was having was primarily based on the shattering of her trust in what she thought she had known, and that she was still on the pathway of learning again how to have faith in her perceptions and judgments. She eventually married again and things worked out well enough. Both she and her sons had, however, been deeply injured by the first husband's glorious breakthrough to freedom, and they suffered its destructive effects in other ways for a very long time.

My second experience that taught me about this form of trauma involved an 18-year-old student who came to me for counseling. He was a very bright young man with deep interests in eastern philosophy and religion, and although he was outwardly functioning well in his college program, he had begun to feel very depressed and wanted someone to talk to about his feelings. I asked him to explain what was depressing him, but he was unable to identify any situation or event that was relevant. He said in fact that really nothing specific was influencing his emotional state, because nothing in his life even seemed completely real. I asked him to explain further what this statement meant, and he said that he felt the world in which he lived was an illusion of some sort, that it lacked any independent reality, and that who he was, or where he was, in actuality, was completely unknown. He said he might be a catatonic schizophrenic locked up in a back ward of some psychiatric hospital, hallucinating his college career and even his conversation with me. Or it seemed possible that some unknown force or God-principle was generating a kind of world-story, and he was a mere character in this cosmic fiction with no independent reality of his own. This sense of everything being some kind of illusion was related to his fascination with the Hindu and Buddhist religions, which are predicated on the idea that the world we sense is Maya or Sangsara, illusory, something from which we need to emancipate ourselves.

The young man's feelings were obviously about something, and I wanted to find out what this might have been. A clue appeared when I asked him how he entertained himself, what he did in his spare time. He told me he liked to hang out in graveyards, by himself. Often late at night, when his family members were already sleeping, he would get in his father's car and drive to one or another of the cemeteries of his town. He liked to walk amongst the gravestones, reading the inscriptions and wondering about the lives of the people who had been buried there. After an hour or so, in each of these visits, he would get back in his car and return home.

How does this relate to epistemological trauma? I let the young man's descriptions of his feelings and practices flow over me like a waterfall. And then I waited for a thought to occur that might take me toward the emotional truth lying inside what had presented itself. The first thought that came was that something must have happened to this person to render the world unreal. One does not come to such an experience for no reason, and so there will always be something that is involved. The second thought that arose was that the nocturnal visitations to the graveyards must be reactions to whatever the event was that turned the world to illusion. It seemed to me that he must be looking for something or someone in the cemeteries, so I asked him what or who this might be. He was not aware of looking for anything specific, however, so he was unable at first to answer my question.

I asked him then if anyone important to him had died, because as I thought about all he was telling me, the word *mourning* kept coming into my mind. He seemed like an aging widower returning to his beloved wife's grave. The sad story of what this was about then came out.

The patient, when he was 7 or 8 years old, had suffered the loss of his mother. He had been very close to her through his earliest years in a family consisting of himself, his mother and father, and three siblings. He was the second-born of the children, and the family's life was one of emotional security and normality. The mother, however, had an undetected temporal lobe cancer. One day, as my patient was at school, a devastating cranial pain occurred, and she collapsed into grave, critical condition. When he came home from school, she was not there, and he was told she had been hospitalized because of a headache but that she would be coming home soon enough, and he was not to worry. He had no reason to doubt what he had been told.

Days passed, the mother did not return, but the boy felt confident that in time everything would work out. Mommy would come back maybe tomorrow or next week when she got well, which again the next-door neighbors had promised him. Incredibly, the boy's father could not face his children and was absent throughout this short period. Finally, one day at school, another child approached the boy and teased him about the fact that his mother had died. My patient struck out at the child who made this seemingly sadistic statement. He was certain his mother was alive, even if not well, and that she would be coming home. After all, he had been told so, and, anyway, mommies don't die. They promise, implicitly and explicitly, that they will always be there.

That night he was informed of the truth by his family's minister. It was disclosed as follows. The minister asked my patient when he thought he would see his mother again. The boy answered, "I don't know, maybe next week or something." The minister then told him he would see her again, but that it would be longer and he would have to wait. The boy asked if it would be a month or more. The minister said no, that he would have to wait longer still. My patient then asked how long it would be. The reply was: "You see, you will be with her again in Heaven. She has died, but in everlasting life, you and she will be reunited." My patient's young heart burst at this point as the awful truth rolled in upon him.

The trauma was twofold. On the one hand he had lost the person to whom he was closest in his life, and continuing without her presence was unthinkable. On the other hand, he had believed and been led to believe that she would get well and return, and this faith in her was foundational for him. But this belief had been shattered, and all that he thought he had known now broke into pieces. It was a trauma of loss, and it was an epistemological trauma of the first magnitude.

Recurrent dreams then appeared as this grieving child lay sleeping. He dreamed dozens of times that his mother was running up to their house and joyfully shouting to everyone that it had all been a misunderstanding, a case of mistaken identity or some such. The dreams were enormously relieving, restoring his mother to life and reconfirming what he had believed was true with all his heart. Upon awakening, however, his beliefs and his mother were lost to him once again. He wept bitterly as he recounted the scene with the minister and told the story of his dreams.

During the weeks following his mother's death, he also tried to have some contact with her spirit, gradually accepting that she had vanished physically but clinging to the belief she was still somehow present, however invisibly and tenuously. He asked her to give him a sign that she was there. Nothing occurred. He then set up a kind of spiritualistic experiment, taking a tiny, almost weightless wisp of cotton, carefully putting it on the surface of one of his mother's sewing thimbles turned upside down, and placing a clear glass over the display to keep drafts of air from disturbing the cotton. Then he waited for his mother's spirit to signal him by moving the wisp, however slightly. The cotton remained still, as motionless as death. Had the experiment worked, he would have known her presence was still real and at least a remnant of all he had believed would have been reconfirmed. Instead, the trauma only continued and deepened.

Within a few months after the tragedy, dissociation set in and the boy stopped thinking about his mother's death and life, throwing himself instead into his schoolwork and experiences with his friends. He wrote an autobiography at the age of 10 for one of his classes and brought it to me during a session. It was remarkable. It recounted a series of incidents belonging to his very early childhood, and then another series belonging to his middle childhood years, but there was no mention of his mother's death, almost as if this part of his history had been excised. He remained aware of the raw physical fact of what had happened, but ceased giving it any thought. Eventually almost all of his memories of his mother's life and death faded from his recall.

I told the patient that I now understood why everything seemed so unreal to him. It was because all that he had considered real had been obliterated in the tragedy of his mother's death. To start with, it had never been conceivable that she could die, so that would be the first blow against what he had believed. And second, he had trusted the reassurances she would return during those anxious days following her hospitalization. So all that was real had been doubly destroyed, and this constituted an attack on the foundation of his world and on his ability to trust his own perceptions. I think this is a primary reason his mother's death had to be dissociated. It was not just the unbearable pain of sadness and missing her that was solved by this adaptation; reality itself was protected against a savage blow, and he was able to continue his young life relatively intact. Intact, that is, until his late teen years as the realness of the world began to be called into question, as everything began to seem increasingly illusory. The walks in the graveyards were transparent efforts to refind his mother, to recover a world that was stolen from him by her death, ultimately to repair and restore an integrity to his own mind and faith in himself.

There had never been an opportunity to share his experiences of loss and invalidation with anyone, and so I tried to create a space within which he could come home to himself. I listened to him as he told of his lonely journey; I stayed with him through a great deal of the crying that occurred; and I told him what I thought had happened to him. That was about it. He understood himself better through this process, which extended over a number of years of our contacts, and he eventually did very well in his life. By the way, one effect of all our discussions was that the reality of the world was restored, and his fascination with Hindu and Buddhist thought receded. He eventually became a clinical psychologist, a very good one.

All trauma is epistemological trauma. My little stories are really just special cases of the more general principle that it belongs to the nature of traumatic experience that it shatters the reality in which the person has believed. It is an attack, in the phrasing of my friend Robert Stolorow (2007), on the "absolutisms of every-day life." The trauma survivor, in consequence, is always someone who has been cast into the darkness of unknowing.

AESTHETICS: THE QUESTION OF THE BEAUTIFUL

Is there a place for the beautiful in how we understand people, perhaps including ourselves? Is the understanding in which we can have faith always beautiful? Are ideas that we develop that seem ugly to the viewer for that reason to be held in doubt? In what, exactly, does beauty in our field consist?

I will go into a specific case and a specific interpretation that emerged in the long course of the patient's psychotherapy. It concerns a dream experienced recurrently by a child between the ages of 5 or 6 and 13. The patient was in her mid-20s when she told me about it, but it was one of the most vivid recollections of her childhood. Here is the dream, in the patient's own words:

> I am lying on my back, naked, in my front yard, staring up into the sky. There are five or six small men lined up on one side of my body, and five or six more on the other side. They seem like gnomes or elves or something. Each one is holding a piece of string in his hands, and on the end of each string, inserted into my skin, is a fishhook. There is one in my cheek, my neck, my breast, my waist, my hip, and down lower on my leg—and the other side of my body the same thing. The men are pulling on their strings and hooks, and my skin, all up and down both sides of my body, is being pulled out and stretched, back and forth. It's a tug-of-war. It's creepy.

There is nothing beautiful on the face of this dream; in fact, it is in its imagery horrifying and ugly. I shall recount how my patient and I came to an understanding of its meaning. It required 13 years. The patient told me the dream on the first occasion I saw her, but neither she nor I could penetrate its opacity. Other dreams she had were easier to understand, but this strange dream of the men with their strings and their hooks floated there for years without any clarification taking place.

The patient, as a small child, had been the victim of the worst sexual abuse I have ever seen. She was enlisted, at the age of 2 or earlier, to provide her father with oral sexual gratification. Two or three times each week, he came into her bedroom, secretly, while other family members were sleeping, and inserted his penis into her mouth. Then he gently encouraged her to stimulate him to erection and eventual orgasm each time. Following this, he would kiss her and tuck her in for a continued night's sleep. The sexual abuse extended over a period of 11 years, at which point it stopped because the father was discovered by a relative in the act of anally raping my patient's younger brother.

Although I knew much about the history of the father's intrusions, I did not understand the connection to the dream until, one night as I sat with my patient, she cried out: "I know what it is! The men, and the strings and the hooks!" She then proceeded to explain that the two rows of little men were images of her two fathers, one of whom was completely normal and the other of whom was a sex maniac. The father of the daylight, as she put it, was a conservative gentleman who supported the family and tried always to represent the highest of moral values. The father of the night, in devastating contrast, was a strange, leering creature who insisted on sexual intimacy and made sure it repeatedly occurred. My patient had dealt with these opposing fathers by cordoning off the experiences in the night from the normal world of the day— when she was in the one she thought nothing about the other. Her development, however, was poised between the two, as she tried to achieve a sense of herself and a life that would have meaning to her in spite of the conflicting pressures and pulls imposed by her father's madness.

I thought my patient's spontaneous interpretation of her dream was beautiful. Perhaps I should say it was not the interpretation that was beautiful, but rather that the dream itself was rendered beautiful *by* the interpretation. Once one understands that the two rows of gnomes symbolize the two worlds of the patient's childhood struggles, the dream becomes a structure beautifully expressing the impossible dilemma in which a young girl finds herself. How perfect the images are: Naked and defenseless she lies there, pulled first to the right, and then to the left, and then again to the right, and the left, and back and forth, endlessly. These movements were the rhythms of her days and nights as she tried to inhabit incompatible realities, created by her father's recurrent turning to her to serve his emotional and sexual needs. The dream is beautiful in that it captures the essence of a child's experience, far better than any rational description could ever hope to. Dreams symbolize the subjective life of the dreamer, and this life was one of feeling forever pulled apart.

This patient also told me she had always felt she was in pieces, as if someone or something long before had pulled her apart. She said her sexuality, her religious beliefs, her humor, her sense of social responsibility, and her competence professionally were all somehow different "selves," none of them connecting to the others in a cohesive structure. She obviously had been pulled apart by the strange double binds implicit in her abuse

I saw her for 30 years, and she did exceptionally well, pulling herself together, marrying and bearing two sons, and progressively freeing herself of the awful legacy of her father's crimes against her. It was in the space of the understanding she and I shared that her ability to surmount the impact of her abuse finally began to crystallize.

If the dream of my patient is made beautiful by the interpretation that sprang into her mind, what accounts for this beauty? In what, precisely, does it consist? The dream becomes beautiful because of the understanding that has emerged. Formerly opaque images that were nothing more than creepy and puzzling suddenly are rendered transparent, and the life dilemmas that are symbolized shine through with breathtaking clarity. Beauty resides in this transparency, in spite of the events that are represented being so terrible. We can look at this strange recurrent dream and feel our hearts breaking in the face of the child's impossible situation.

The tragic inner truth of this young life is inscribed in the dreams, and truth and beauty go hand in hand.

When we understand something about someone, and what I have called "the inner truth" of a life becomes disclosed, does this always entail an experience of the beautiful? I think the sensation of beauty resides precisely in the perception of truth. A case on which I consulted recently comes to mind, but really any time one reaches an understanding of a life one will find an instance of what I am talking about.

The story I think of involves another young man, a 22-year-old philosophy student pursuing his doctorate. I was called upon as a consultant by his analyst, herself a young woman. He was a self-described radical determinist. This meant that he felt and believed there to be no such thing as freedom. He argued, with great passion, that all talk of choice, of agency, of volition was nonsense, because the structure and content of our lives is controlled by our circumstances. Human beings are, according to the position he maintained, 100% in the grip of their history of conditioning and of their biological evolution.

Another aspect of what this man argued was that true communication between people is impossible, because everyone is locked up in his or her private subjectivity. One could not dispute any of this without becoming the target of a withering refutation.

A final feature of the case was that he said he expected to kill himself before his 30th birthday. There was absolutely no reason to live, as far as he was concerned, but he did find philosophical argumentation mildly amusing, and so his suicide was postponed for a few years while he pursued and promoted his determinism. He said he might write a book expounding his ideas, and then celebrate its publication by ending his life.

I saw no beauty in this young man's thinking at first; in fact, the ideas were rather ugly and bleak. The analyst consulting with me had been drawn into debates with the young man about his philosophy, and the resulting arguments had become heated and disturbing. It was obvious that such an approach would be fruitless, in part because the patient was so brilliant and quick that he could run circles around almost anyone. Those whose intellectual positions he successfully countered became objects of scorn to him, and the analysis was at risk of failing before it even began. This was the reason for the consultation.

I told the analyst about certain feelings and images that came into my mind as I listened to the summary of the patient's philosophical convictions. I was letting the waterfall flow again. The first feeling was of sadness, as I thought about the vision of people as isolated prisoners of their own private subjectivity. Sadness, and then an intense lonely feeling enveloped me, and I went on from there to a sense of powerlessness and helplessness, as I thought about his determinism. An image formed that was very clear, of a little boy, a miserable child whose isolation was profound and who felt unable to have any effect on the people in his surroundings. It was a picture of a depressed youth who was misunderstood and abandoned by his parents and other family members. I urged the analyst to let herself flow in a similar direction in an effort to find the emotional meaning of this man's dark philosophy. An idea then came to us that his rigorous, aggressive arguments on behalf of his thinking were highly intellectualized efforts to control and master an underlying life tragedy.

I asked about the man's mother and father. He had briefly explained in his first meeting with the analyst that he did not know his parents. He had lived with them, in their house, but they were people who never expressed any affection, physically or verbally. Wholly undemonstrative and uncommunicative, they had made their son feel like he was living with strangers. These same strangers, nevertheless, had been oddly involved and over-involved with many of his experiences and choices growing up. His father, hearing of his early interests in philosophy when he was a high school student, contacted various colleges for him to consider attending. His father also arranged a summer internship after high school graduation where he could work in a philosophy professor's office.

There was more. A part of the family saga concerned what had happened to the young man's father when he, the father, had been a boy. He had shown signs of great talent in drawing and painting as a young child, and had made a very early decision that his destiny was to become an artist. This deeply held intention, however, had not gone over well with his own father, who, after tolerating the artistic interests for a few years, insisted that it was all effeminate foolishness and needed to be given up. When there was resistance against this decision, all the art supplies were taken away, and the will of the boy was summarily crushed. The mother did not come to her son's defense. He never painted or drew again, and later became a certified public accountant.

The thought ran through my mind: What if the patient's father was, in his heart and soul, an artist though? Then it could be said that he was spiritually killed by his own father, because it is my view that an artist is nothing other than his art. I wondered if this man was somehow trying to reconstitute his own destroyed life in the journey of his son, my colleague's patient. What if the father had saddled his son with the task of living out his own unfulfilled life? The analyst said there had been some further features of the young man's history that were indeed consistent with such an understanding. The father had personally arranged multiple employment opportunities, college and graduate school admissions, and had even written his son's personal statements and résumé. Although he was emotionally unconnected to the boy, he had done everything for him to such an extent that the patient needed only to flow into the slots that kept being prearranged for him. Hearing this, the philosophical determinism that had previously seemed so unattractive began to glow with a strange beauty in my eyes. His arguments—that agency and volition are illusions and that people are deterministic pawns—perfectly crystallized the experience of a child whose life has been created for him, prescripted and therefore predetermined in every detail. Every detail, that is, except for one: the determinism itself, which now appeared to me to be the lonely cry of a soul in bondage.

I suggested that when the young man launched into long intellectual disquisitions, she tell him she had images of an isolated, lonely boy that came into her mind. When he told of how human beings are determined and how free will is an illusion, she could speak of a child who had no say in the unfolding course of his own little life. I suggested she could even make use of some of his fancy vocabulary in this refocusing of their conversations, by telling him he seemed to have been raised by a couple of windowless monads. His parents were like that: people whose inner experiences were completely inaccessible. I would anticipate such reactions would bring a halt to the philosophizing and make contact instead with the underlying emotion. I would want to see the young man crying. If he could be brought into the feelings beneath his very depressing philosophy, there was a good chance that his planned suicide could be averted. People often need, above all other things, to cry.

It all came together more or less as I had hoped. The young man, when responded to on the basis of his inner feelings, dropped his intellectualizing philosophy and began to sob. He cried long and hard, for hours and days and weeks. Eventually an idea crystallized out of all this sadness, an idea within his own mind about all that he had lost in the course of his journey from childhood to genius. He had lost the opportunity, reduced to its simplest terms, to be himself. He had lost the chance to grow into the person he might otherwise have become: the hopeful, creative young man who could give of his fundamentally loving nature to others. I don't want to make this sound all positive— there has been an enduring legacy of bitterness about the absence of support in his original family, and as well about the pervasive absence of support in our society for authenticity in the lives of its citizens. Still and all, he came out as someone who could support community rather than isolation, the expression of individual identity in a sustaining social world. I would say this was quite an achievement, in view of the cynical, deadly philosophy from which it began.

4

Dreams and Delusions

[In a dream, a delusion, or a work of art] a situation taken up into a metaphor loses its transitory, painful and unstable quality, and becomes full of significance and inner validity, the moment it passes wholly into an image.

Rainer Maria Rilke

I first discovered the field of psychology, during my 17th year, in the writings of Freud and Jung. Among the many intriguing things with which these gentlemen concerned themselves, I discovered, was the world of dreams and dream interpretation. Nothing has ever been more interesting to me. What follows is a collection of ideas and clinical stories about the dreaming process and the use of dream interpretation in psychotherapy. I also take up the relationship between dreams and delusions.

THE MAN WHOSE HEAD WAS CRUSHED BY WALT DISNEY

In a psychoanalytic seminar during the years of my training, the instructor presented the idea that one should always pay close attention to the very first dream a patient presents in psychotherapy. It was his opinion that this first dream will concern the deepest theme of the treatment that is to come, often forecasting or otherwise symbolizing the content of a process extending over many years. I found this idea interesting, and it has largely been borne out in my own clinical experiences. I shall begin with an account of one such dream, the terrifying nightmare of a young man who came to me for analysis a long time ago. This patient, 35 years old, was a teacher at a small college, and was suffering with a serious depression. After our first meeting, he sent a note describing his dream, which became a centerpiece of our work together. These were his exact words:

> I watched a teenage boy walking into a large room. He had suffered a permanently damaging cerebral injury, in an earlier fall from a swing. He approached a table behind which sat an array of older men, and in the center, kind of like the chairman of the board, was Walt Disney. On the table were various small objects: pens, coffee cups, keys. The boy concentrated on these things and, psychokinetically, made them begin to whirl, levitate, and move up and down the table. It was a dazzling demonstration of paranormal powers. Walt Disney reached over the table and gently cupped the boy's head in both his hands. This affectionate holding continued for a few moments, but then Disney began to press inward. Very slowly the pressure increased, moment by moment, and finally, with an exertion of enormous strength, the boy's head collapsed and was horrifyingly pulverized.

As I read the text, it became evident my patient was giving me his autobiography, a story in which severe trauma played a repeating role. Strangely, he had no understanding of this. He was someone who skated along the surface of his very painful experiences, unmindful of the extremity of the things he had faced.

Dreams are autobiographical microcosms, symbolizing the subjective life of the dreamer. They are representations, to ourselves, of all that we undergo and all that we feel. Here a life is pictured involving a fall and injury, the appearance of magical powers, the finding of a loving embrace from a person of authority, and then a deadly crushing by that figure. My patient did not regard the dream as anything more than an odd puzzle of impressions and symbols, and the only remark he made was that the

Disney figure might have represented the pressure he sometimes put on himself.

I told him what I thought: that it was a metaphorical account of his emotional history, of injuries that had occurred, of the lastingly disabling blow of something symbolized by the fall from a swing, and later something else, represented by the violence of Walt Disney. I did not know the specific events of this man's life, but I was sure I was seeing the effects of his history vividly portrayed. I asked him to tell me what had hurt him so deeply. He could not respond. Finally he told me that there was a strange pressure, like a soft elastic band or a cloth, drenched in warm water, somehow wrapped around his head, pressing gently and covering his eyes. It was the pressure of sorrow he carried in his heart, an indescribable sadness that was with him at all times. This man was one of the saddest people I have ever known, and it was interesting to me that he seemed not to be aware of it as such. His experience was just one of wet, warm pressure, as if he had been crying. What was the history in this case represented by the events of this man's dream? There had been an early fall of a kind, a violent blow that made him feel changed forever. His mother, someone deeply beloved by him, had died very suddenly because of an undiagnosed brain tumor when he was 8 years old. After long discussions with me, he was able to recall what he had felt upon learning of her death: He had been as if impaled on a pole, which some terrible force was swinging violently back and forth in the sky and slamming him into the ground again and again.

The dream included an idea that there had been a fall from a swing and a brain injury—an allusion to the impact of the death, which as a boy he had pictured as extreme violence. So the first part of the dream seemed to condense the early trauma history. I was unable to specifically decode the idea of a fall from a swing, until he remembered being swung through the sky and slammed into the earth. The paranormal powers that appear are a kind of inverse of his trauma; they create an image in which debilitating effects are undone by supernatural capabilities. As I contemplated this young man's impressive powers in the dream, a deep sadness came over me. He can move things around with his mind, but he cannot undo the injury that precedes it. He creates miraculous effects upon the small objects lying before him on the table, but he cannot bring his mother back from the dead. A binary crystallizes here: supernatural potency versus utter helplessness, the kind of thing one sees often enough with shattering trauma.

The psychokinesis also stands in relation to the third part of the dream, wherein Walt Disney cradles, and then pulverizes, the young man's head. These images, I saw immediately, tell a further story of something that had happened, something crushing. I told him that I thought someone had hurt him really badly, and I asked who it was. He answered that he didn't know, and wondered again if this concerned terrible demands he put on himself. Again I posed my question: "Who is it that first of all showed a protective, supportive love, but then exerted some kind of brutalizing pressure on you?"

He finally answered differently, describing a recent letter from an admired older man, someone who had been his beloved mentor but who had turned on him and on his work and teaching at his college. Years earlier, my patient, a brand-new Ph.D., had met a senior faculty member in his department, a gentleman who was an internationally recognized scholar in my patient's field of study. An intellectual love affair had developed between them, in which the scholar mirrored and nurtured the emerging talents of my patient, and my patient devoted himself to supporting the creative work and thinking of his mentor. The first years of this relationship were idyllic, and the native capabilities of the young man began to unfold into important ideas and writings. It is possible that the dream picture of paranormal abilities alludes to these evolving capacities, which, to the young man, seemed like miracles brought into being by his inspiring mentor. Again and again he found that in the presence of the older man, in dialogues about various ideas and developments in their shared field, insights would come into his mind that he could never have achieved while working alone.

As he continued to develop under this nurturing guidance, he began to publish on a number of topics, and his field began to recognize a new voice that had appeared in its midst.

Here is where the problem arose: The older man could not tolerate the success of my patient, when he had sown the seeds of that success but was now receiving no public credit. My patient saw clearly his indebtedness to his mentor, and even tried to coauthor a number of essays and books with him. But the older man did not approve of all the directions in which the work was going, and a collaborative enterprise turned out not to be possible. In the meantime, the mentoring professor's own scholarship had become paralyzed, and he had published nothing over a period of many years. But now he was witnessing the development of ideas he had participated in inspiring, in the works of the young man he had nurtured. A paranoia began to crystallize, in which the older one visualized the younger one as a kind of vampire, feeding off of his thoughts and stealing all his most important concepts. Finally, in a rage, the mentor fired off a long letter filled with ugly accusations, telling my patient he had cannibalized a treasure house of original ideas in order to satisfy a pathological need for fame. He also communicated his suspicions to important figures in his field, and this began to come back over the grapevine to my patient. The accusation of intellectual robbery, spread across the country, was experienced as a crushing personal blow, and this is certainly what is symbolized in the horrible violence with which his bad dream comes to an end.

I worked with him closely, and he eventually did reasonably well. He found it possible to partially heal the breach, basically by flooding the older man with letters and phone calls of love and gratitude. After a number of years, things improved between them, and the mentor finally expressed forgiveness and regret for how he had reacted. This softened the blow of the trauma significantly. It also helped my patient to learn that other students of his mentor had experienced the same thing: an initial period of nurturance followed by accusations of robbery and extreme hostility when the students sought to break away and find their own pathways.

Why was it that the person in the dream administering the crushing blow was Walt Disney? I don't know. My patient disliked Walt Disney, and regarded his lifework as plastic and artificial—although he said he did have a fondness in his heart for Scrooge McDuck.

It occurred to me that Walt Disney fed the fantasies of the young, entertaining them with all manner of stories having magical and supernatural qualities. But he was also a man exploiting the sense of enchantment among children to achieve commercial success. In this respect he was rather like the Wizard of Oz, appearing magical, until one discovers his all-too-human failings. Similarly the mentor figure was idealized, until he too revealed his own personal limitations—by attacking my patient for stealing away fame and recognition. He continued to love his mentor for many years. He also continued to feel a certain amount of pain about the events that had transpired, being haunted in particular by the "forgiveness" that had been granted—implying he was still being seen as having committed a crime.

I did not focus on this young man's associations in determining what the dream imagery might concern. Is this not a cardinal principle of psychoanalytic dream interpretation? Here is what I think, after half a century of studying dreams and their meanings. Interpreting a dream is a matter of locating the context of experience to which it belongs. Sometimes a dreamer's associations can assist in this, but often the associations are misleading. My patient's thoughts went in the direction of the harsh judgments he placed on himself. This was not entirely unrelated to the dream, but strayed from the heart of the matter: He had been terribly hurt by what had happened to him. An ongoing issue for him was that he seemed to move along the edge of his own painful feelings. The dream, in contrast, presents two images involving great violence: first a fall, leading to irreversible brain damage; and second, the crushing of a person's head. So we could say the dream stands up for the extremity of his historical experiences, correcting or compensating for his conscious attitude of unmindfulness.

THE ELECTROCUTION OF A BABY GIRL

I will now tell a story about a second patient's initial dream in a long psychotherapy process that occurred. The account concerns a 31-year-old woman who sought help because of paralyzing feelings of being a frightened child, lost in a world of high-powered grownups. These disruptive states stood in contrast to her external situation, one of having achieved great financial success and of having earned the respect of numbers of people who followed her leadership. She was an impressive adult by every objective criterion, but her feelings were of being a terrified little girl. Here is the dream as she presented it, which occurred the night following our first meeting:

> I am walking down a long corridor toward a brightly illuminated room. As I approach the doorway, I see a baby girl, not more than a year old. She is sitting on a blanket in the middle of the floor, and there is a strange metal contraption on her head. It seems to be a helmet of some sort, with coiled wires coming out of the top and connecting into a wall. A horrible realization: The baby is about to be electrocuted, and the helmet and wires are part of the apparatus that will kill her. Doomed.

The dream was one of terror. I understood it as her picture of her situation in entering into a psychotherapy relationship. She felt she was submitting herself to something that would end her life. What this awful expectation came from only became clear when she added a detail regarding the dream, some weeks later. The infant on the blanket had been naked, facing the door, with her little legs spread apart. This baby was wide open to some kind of sexual attack.

She had undergone a terrible sexual exploitation, perpetrated against her by an earlier psychotherapist. The story was this: She had known, loved, and trusted a man, who had helped her during her late teen years with deeply buried feelings arising out of extreme neglect and abuse in her family of origin. But then, having earned her devotion over a 3-year period, he changed the terms of their tie: It now became her responsibility to keep him sexually satisfied. He presented the new arrangement with an explanation that their sexual interaction would help her crystallize her emerging identity as a mature woman. She had absolute faith in this gentleman, who she believed had saved her life, and therefore complied. For more than a year she provided oral gratification on a regular basis, and even paid for the opportunity, because of its ostensible purpose of solidifying her flowering womanhood. Finally, when she began to express doubt and confusion, he became angry and denounced her for being too childish to appreciate the incomparable gift she was receiving. She then fled the relationship, vowing never again to depend on anyone.

She reburied the child within her, along with the deep hurt to her soul. Although she knew she could never return to him, she maintained an idealized picture of their relationship that encapsulated all the good things he had given to her before the sexual interaction commenced. In the ensuing years, she completed her education and rose within her profession to a very high level of competence and responsibility. It was at this point that the injured child began to resurface, in the form of feeling like a little girl surrounded by scary grownups. She needed help in the worst way, but to seek help from a psychotherapist was to reenter the danger zone that had already nearly killed her. She was afraid that by entering into a new psychotherapy she was signing her own death warrant.

As in the case of the young man I described earlier, I told the patient what I thought the dream meant. I explained that I found the terror in her heart was understandable, in view of what had happened in the other psychotherapy. I also suggested that she might have begun to trust me already, and that this was what was causing the surge of fear. Look at what trusting an analyst before had brought into her life. She was telling me that if the same thing happened this time, it would be the end.

Working with such patients is always difficult, because trust needs to become established; but trust has become a deadly enemy. So one goes back and forth, often for a long time; eventually though things tend to work out if there is a shared understanding of the storms of fear that arise.

Why did she have this dream? Why not just say how afraid she was? The dream was her way of telling me of her fear. The original experience of having been injured by her therapist had actually never fully developed. It was dissociated after her departure from the relationship, and in the early months of our work she still idealized this man. A positive picture of his meaning in her life was indispensable to her continuing survival and progress. The fullness of his damage to her life became real to her only very slowly. But the dream registered that damage vividly right at the beginning. There is an old idea in our field that the disaster one fears in the future is actually a memory of a catastrophe that occurred long ago. This would seem to apply here, in the frightening picture of the impending murder of a baby girl.

If my patient had been in touch with how deeply hurt she was, I think there would not have been a need for a dream. Dreams capture something that is incomplete in one's conscious life. Impressions, feelings, memories, thoughts all in a swirl, not worked out, insufficiently articulated, incompletely thought through: This is the stuff of dreaming.

Freud (1900/2004) gave us the formulation that every dream fulfills a wish, or attempts to do so. How would my own formulation about the general features of dreams relate to his? Freud was hypnotized by the image of the unfulfilled wish. One could reinterpret his proposal as a special case of the more general principle that dreams are attempts to resolve subjective tensions. They express a need to come to terms with issues that are problematic in the waking life of the dreamer. There are obviously many situations that are laden with tension other than the one involving an unfulfilled wish.

DREAMS AND DELUSIONS

In my youth, enamored of Freud and Jung, I had the idea that the study of dreams and their meanings might disclose profound truths about human existence. Here are my thoughts on this matter, after dwelling on the issue for a very long time.

It is human nature to dream, which means to create systems of symbols representing our ongoing subjective life. Our consciousness itself, in consequence, becomes immensely more complex than would be the case if we lived only in unsymbolized immediacy. In our evolution, humanity came to itself when dreaming began. It is a foundational manifestation of the symbolic capacity, and it is this that distinctively defines human nature. One may ask if dreams can somehow teach us the secret of human nature. The fact that dreams exist is human nature showing itself.

What is my understanding of the relationship between dreams and language? Many have thought that it is language that defines the uniqueness of human beings. Dreams and language appeared together. They are coequal manifestations of the symbolic function. I place the capacity for creative symbolization at the center of human existence, and dreams are a cardinal expression of this capacity.

Returning to the dreams discussed earlier, the first about the young man whose head was crushed, and the second about the infant's electrocution, can it be said that these images are matters of creative symbolization? The creativity involved in those two instances is breathtaking, transforming emotional injuries into dramatic events. In one case someone's devastation at the hands of his beloved mentor is represented as the sadistic crushing of a boy's skull. In the other, the searing transformation of a therapist into an exploitive monster is visualized as the impending murder by electrocution of a baby girl. Dreams are quintessentially creative, which is one of the reasons I think they are central sources of culture itself. Also, dreams are not just a matter of the play of images in discrete intervals during our hours of sleeping; we are continuously dreaming, daydreaming, fantasizing, and playing, and symbolizations of subjective life are always crystallizing, interlacing, and interacting with one another.

But let us turn to a different question: What is the relationship between dreams and delusions? Are they the same thing? Is a delusion a dream from which one cannot awaken?

Engaging with these questions requires first of all a definition of the term *delusion*. The conventional definition is that it is a false belief someone clings to in spite of all contrary rational argument and evidence. Drawing on the principles of phenomenological contextualism, I would say a delusion is a belief, any belief, about the validity of which there can be no discussion. The evaluation that the belief is false requires a comparison between what is real to the person and what is real according to some objective, external standard—a dilemma one can avoid by staying with the idea that there can be no discussion of the validity of the so-called delusional belief.

So what then can we conclude from a comparison of dreams and delusions? A delusion is similar to a dream in that it is an enveloping experience with little or no reflective awareness. One can compare and contrast the two with regard to the contexts involved. The context of dreaming, whether in sleep or in reverie, is one in which attention becomes unfocused; thought frees itself from the constraints of logic and reason; experiences are cast into concrete perceptual images; and everything becomes more or less interchangeable with everything else. Freud offered an idea about this in his theory of the so-called primary process. I prefer not to use his terminology, but he was right to emphasize there are differences in the organization of our thoughts and experiences in different states of mind.

So-called delusions share certain features with dreams: They partake of the concretizations dreams show; their organization follows no logical or rational schema; and things become interchangeable with each other in all kinds of complex ways. A delusion, though, is a generally stable structure, and in this respect is like a dream from which one does not awaken. Another resemblance has to do with memory: Delusions, when they recede, tend to be forgotten, almost as if they had never been there, like a dream that lingers for a while but then fades into oblivion.

Delusions form, generally speaking, in a context of very severe threats against a person's sense of existing: They belong to the psychology of annihilation states. By casting the danger to a person's sense of being in highly concrete, particular images, the delusion expresses an effort to resurrect oneself and be protected from the possibility of obliteration. Someone in the midst of these struggles may have a dream that essentially does the same thing, and that dream may carry over into a relatively permanent structure, which we would then call a delusion. So a delusion could be understood as a long-lasting dream, elaborated in the context of personal annihilation.

The story of Anna returns to mind, whose experiences I touched upon in chapter 1. She was the young woman who had a terrible dream of being shot by her mother as she, Anna, stood before a large mirror. The result of the shooting was that the glass of the mirror disintegrated into a swirling cloud of fragments, and the patient became nothing more than a fleeting, vanishing shadow. This dream, vividly symbolizing an experience of personal annihilation, was helpful in decoding the subjective truths inhering in the patient's persecutory delusions about penetrating, killing rays attacking her from the eyes of her enemies. These rays, it will be recalled, began at a certain point of the therapy to emanate from my own eyes, producing all manner of difficult reactions from Anna and threatening the work in which she and I were engaged.

The dream and the delusion displayed an isomorphic relation to one another: In both instances, an invasive, penetrating action from without was followed by a sense of being killed and erased from being. There actually was an array of other similarly structured images Anna became afflicted by in this early period of her therapy. For example, she repeatedly became convinced that tiny insects, perhaps ticks, had somehow crawled into the canals of her ears and were voraciously eating their ways deep into her brain. Medical examinations revealed no problems in her ears or in her brain. Her drawings at that time also seemed to reflect experiences of being intruded upon and invaded. She produced dozens of images showing a person with his face pressed up against hers, in such a way that the other's long, pointed nose was piercing her face and head, intruding into the inner structure of her brain. The drawings were horrifying to look at: They seemed to depict a bizarre, brutalizing rape of my patient's head. All of these representations—in her dream, her delusion, her fearful fantasy of the invading insects, and her artwork—gave concrete form to a feeling of being usurped and annihilated by the intrusive, invalidating perceptions and attributions of others. Perhaps the worst of these experiences occurred in a psychiatric context, wherein she was relentlessly viewed as a deeply disturbed schizophrenic.

The ultimate extreme of the destruction materialized in her psychotherapy with me, when my uncomprehending reactions to her delusional preoccupations made her feel herself turning into an incomprehensible psychiatric object, a dead thing composed of neural solidities produced by the rays flowing out of my eyes. With the help of her dream, as well as of her other images, I finally saw the impact of my invalidations on her capacity to feel an ongoing sense of being. This in turn made possible a new response to her devastation and, finally, our relationship became something that began to sustain rather than destroy her.

The dream of the obliterating gunshot and the delusion of the petrifying rays from others' eyes thus were equivalents of each other, concretely depicting her failing struggle to maintain a sense of being alive in the midst of forces that, from her point of view, made such survival impossible.

In this story, a dream and its context helped to decode the metaphor present in a delusion. I shall now tell another one in which the relationship between a dream and a delusion can again be illuminated. Is there a general principle that can be stated connecting the one to the other? Let us consider the dream and principal delusion of the famous patient, Renee, the author of *Autobiography of a Schizophrenic Girl* (Sechehaye, 1951). I will quote the young woman's words describing her dream.

> A barn, brilliantly illuminated by electricity. The walls painted white, smooth—smooth and shining. In the immensity, a needle—fine, pointed, hard, glittering in the light. The needle in the emptiness filled me with excruciating terror. Then a haystack fills up the emptiness and engulfs the needle. The haystack, small at first, swells and swells and in the center, the needle, endowed with tremendous electrical force, communicates its charge to the hay. The electrical current, the invasion by the hay, and the blinding light combine to augment the fear to a paroxysm of terror and I wake up screaming. (p. 21)

It seems to me that Renee was identified with the needle, and the engulfing hay that fills the brightly illuminated barn was a symbol of the annihilation experience she was undergoing. The surrounding passages in her book describe a progressively deepening derealization experience, in which everything around her began to appear mechanical, separated into isolated single elements. It was a breakdown of the coherence of her world and a loss of the sense that anything was real. The swelling, engulfing hay expressed a feeling of being consumed by unreality.

Why did Renee use the image of the needle? The thought that comes to mind is that the needle must have been phallic, masculine, and probably symbolized what remained of her sense of agentic selfhood. A female's representation of herself as male also suggests an active disidentification with the feminine, a distancing from the figure of the mother, and therefore alludes implicitly to maternal disasters in her family of origin.

The electrical current inside the needle is almost certainly the sensation of pure terror in the face of the annihilation that was occurring. That is what terror feels like: an intensifying electrical current passing through one's body, and its communication to the hay shows that her universe was becoming completely pervaded by it. This was an experience of a fall into the abyss of madness.

One could ask what would be the circumstances in a child's life that could produce the annihilation state from which Renee was suffering. If someone feels his or her world and selfhood are being destroyed, then something has happened to produce that. Such feelings do not emerge from nothing; they come about in a human context involving an absolute catastrophe. One would need to look at her early years, at the qualities of her relationships to caregivers—although I don't think anyone gave her much care based on looking at this dream and its probable meanings. I would expect to find a story of neglect, of rejection, of abuse, of invalidation, perhaps of exploitation. Such a state could only come about because of some truly awful things having happened.

Consider now Renee's delusion and let us see if some further formulation of the relation between dreams and delusions emerges in our discussion. I will give a description, again in her words. It concerns a machine that became a relentless persecutor:

> I constructed an electric machine to blow up the earth and everyone with it. But what was even worse, with the machine I would rob all men of their brains, thus creating robots obedient to my will alone. This was my greatest, most terrible revenge. (p. 35)

There was an all-engulfing feeling of guilt, without definition and focus. A crime had been committed, but one had no idea what it was, and the punishment for this crime was a feeling of everlasting culpability. Although the electrical device began as a weapon against others, it quickly transformed into a malign entity that attacked Renee. She described the source of her guilt, which was somehow equivalent to the machine, as the "System": the supreme persecutor of her world. All humanity was the victim of this persecution, and those who became aware of this she referred to as "Enlightened."

The System also began to exact punishment by ordering her to burn her hand. To obey such orders, according to her account, would not bring an end to the persecution, however; it would only increase its power and intensify the agony of her guilt. So what about this so-called System? What exactly is it, and how can we understand the relationship between its persecutory action and her dream of the needle and the hay?

Renee's delusion of the System is a counterpart to the engulfing hay in the dream. The hay threatened to swallow up and obliterate the electrified needle, which is a symbol of the annihilation of all sense of personal identity by the onrush of unreality that was afflicting her. The System also surrounded Renee and threatened to disrupt and erase her personal individuality, by usurping her will and inducing actions of extreme self-destructiveness. The System reminds me of Kafka's *The Trial* (1925/1998), which is also about a strange, all-consuming guilt.

I would say Renee's crime, like Kafka's, was that she tried to exist as a person in her own right. There were experiences in her background that undermined her chance to develop a sense of her own selfhood and of her own world as real. Perhaps, in addition to whatever abuse she suffered, there were pressures to make her serve the needs of caregivers. Then we could understand the System as a concretization of the actual family context, including Renee's compliant surrender to the agendas that were imposed. Within such a system, to claim a life of one's own is indeed a crime. Often, though, this sort of thing takes place silently, unnoticed, and even the developing child whose soul is being taken does not see the violence that is occurring, that is, until suddenly there is a hostile persecutor engaging in unspeakable acts. The violence against the child thereby breaks into consciousness, in the form of strange paranoid visions like Renee's—or in great works of art, such as Kafka's famous novel. The delusion therefore carries the subjective truth of a young woman's life history, and it expresses her fight to prevent that history from destroying her.

This shows again, as in my other example, how the annihilation experience in a psychotic state appears in dreams and obviously also in a patient's so-called delusions. Sometimes they are closely similar to each other; in other instances the imagery is very different. I would not want to make too much of a distinction between these classes of experiences. For all I know, Renee's electric machine that turns into her persecutor may have originated as a dream to start with. Dreams depict the subjective life of the dreamer, and so do delusions.

Given the nature of Renee's struggle, what sort of psychotherapy approach can we envision? The book tells the story of the treatment, which was completely successful, and I could not improve on the process that is described. Renee's analyst, Margarite Sechehaye, made a profound commitment to her patient and worked closely and lovingly with her over a period of many years. That is what is needed in such cases.

5

The Unbearable and the Unsayable

You want me to call up
Something so desperate that the thought of it
Wrings my heart before my tongue can speak.

Dante
The Inferno

I was recently speaking with a noted psychoanalyst, and he told me that clinicians generally do not understand something important about the impact of trauma—that it changes the structure of a person's brain, permanently. According to this idea, he further explained, certain pathways of excitation and reaction are laid down "in the neurological substrate" by very severe trauma, and once this has occurred, the person is altered biologically and the central nervous system responds differently, forevermore. It was implicit in his thinking that psychoanalytic exploration would never be capable, in itself, of affecting these supposedly permanent alterations. If such an idea is true, it would appear to set limits on the applicability of psychoanalysis to those many conditions in which severe trauma plays a role.

What is one to do with a claim such as this one? It was offered in a very sober tone, as if there were solid scientific evidence in its support. In working with severe trauma survivors, do we need to be concerned with their altered, damaged nervous systems? Should clinicians explain to their patients that their brains have been permanently affected? It is difficult to imagine that this would be other than a very destructive thing to say to someone. It is also hard to see how one would substantiate an idea like this—it being very crude, and actually more of a fantasy than a scientific hypothesis: a neurological fantasy. It does have a meaning, however: The image of irreversible changes in the brain is probably a reification of certain feelings that lie at the heart of trauma.

What are the experiences that are being reified in such imagery? It is a matter of a person's sense that he or she has been irrevocably changed by what has occurred. It is the feeling that one will never be the same again. A person undergoing such a feeling might have a dream of his or her brain having been permanently damaged or modified, but taking such an image literally, as my psychoanalytic colleague seems to have done, is not anything one should become terribly serious about. It may be that this reification serves in part as a means of neutralizing the devastating power of trauma. My colleague, it is no surprise, was himself a serious trauma victim: early physical and emotional abuse in his family, and multiple medical crises later that devastated his whole childhood. The theorists of trauma in our field are often victims of trauma in their histories, and the ways in which they have found to survive their emotional injuries leave an imprint on the ideas that then become current in our work. It would be good if clinicians and writers would think deeply about such connections.

Reification in this instance is the transformation, in imagination, of a subjective experience into a material thing. It is the symbolization of something felt, in a concrete image, and then simultaneously the loss of the sense of the symbolic as the image is recast as existing in physical reality. The disturbing, nebulous feeling of having been somehow irrevocably altered is replaced by a compelling vision of a physical change in the nervous system. By concretizing an otherwise terrifying sense of no longer even being the same person one has been, the feeling of personal disruption and discontinuity is diminished and encapsulated to some extent. People like to nail down such things that happen to them in specific, localized physical images, and that is exactly what is occurring here. It is kind of sad, though, when one sees these processes unconsciously giving rise to supposed psychological and physiological "theories." Such theories never take us anywhere, except away from the intensity of the experiences they are presented to explain.

TRAUMA AND DISSOCIATION

What is the nature of the change that occurs when a person passes through a traumatic experience, but then seems not to know that he or she has done so? How does it come to pass that someone develops an amnesia for an event that has transpired? The best definition of dissociation that I have found was offered by one of my own patients, a woman who had been a victim, as a young child, of a long series of atrocious sexual assaults. The memories of these terrible events vanished as she grew up, and she only began to reclaim them after many years of psychotherapy and also after finding and marrying a man who made her feel loved and accepted. Some 15 years into the process of recalling and reliving her vast trauma, she one day remarked to me: "You know, George, I guess I just became someone none of this had ever happened to."

A person who has amnesia for some emotionally traumatic event just has the amnesia, and that is it. He or she doesn't remember it. In fact, as far as that person is concerned, it never occurred. The person becomes someone in whose life the event did not happen. That is what dissociation is.

How can a person become someone something did not happen to? Can it be said that this involves a splitting of consciousness? Consciousness does not and cannot split. It is not a material thing. Only material objects, like diamonds, can split. The person becomes someone for whom the incident did not take place, and nothing more. There is a tradition in our field that pictures consciousness as undergoing such splits: vertical splits, horizontal splits, dissociations that segregate one nucleus of experience from another. These images are all concretizing reifications, rather like the supposed brain changes referred to earlier; they refer to nothing objectively real, and they explain absolutely nothing. They are symbols we use to represent and master experiences that are beyond our capacity to assimilate.

Something happens in someone's life. It is too much for the person to bear, so it is not borne. It is too much to be put into words, so nothing is said. It is too much to even be aware of, so awareness vanishes. The person has become someone for whom it did not occur. Of course, the person is nevertheless affected by the incident, whether or not he or she knows of its existence. The events of our lives have all kinds of effects on us, regardless of whether those events are accessible to our conscious recollection.

In a conference on trauma and dissociation I recently attended, I was asked about my views on so-called dissociative identity disorder, also known as multiple personality. I answered that I had no "views" on multiplicity: It is a phenomenon one encounters from time to time, and that is all. The questioner continued to press on, explaining that some people in our field say it is real and is generated by severe childhood trauma, most often including sexual violations; other people say it is a fiction, created by overly zealous therapists working with suggestible, compliant patients. I was asked for my position on this debate.

I am not a believer in any "real" phenomenon of multiplicity, if I understand what this word means to those who use it in this context; nor do I subscribe to the oversimplified notion of anything being "induced." These are false alternatives: the first assigning the essence of so-called dissociative identity disorder exclusively to the patient, and the second to the influencing therapist. Multiplicity comes into being, in all its glory, at the interface of patient and analyst, and both make their contributions. It is neither independently real, nor is it unilaterally induced. A person with a history of unbearable, unsayable trauma comes into a developing connection with someone—perhaps an analyst, but it could be anyone—and depending on the kind of response this person encounters, the trauma history may begin to emerge in the form of a flowering of seemingly autonomous alters. It is also possible no such emergence will take place, and the history will remain mute.

I had an experience many years ago with one such patient that taught me much about this matter. A 45-year-old woman called me for a consultation regarding her ongoing psychotherapy. She had been in analysis for 8 years with a well-known figure in our field. She said she was unhappy with the results of her treatment and needed advice on what to do about it. I asked her to tell me about her relationship with her analyst as well as about her background. As a child she had been the victim of profound sexual abuse by her mother, who had used her relentlessly during her early years as a masturbation toy. She said that there had once been "some boys." A question came into my mind, and I decided to voice it. I asked her what the names of the boys were. She said she did not recall, and also the boys were gone and it was all a long time ago. Then another thought came to me, and again I decided to express it. I told her I thought it wasn't a very nice thing to forget a person's name. She was quiet for a moment, and then she said: "I think you are a mother. That is the whole problem in my analysis—my analyst is only a father. He always wants me to be grown up and reasonable."

As we spoke about her dilemma, the names of the boys began to come back to her. Finally, she told me that the boys had not disappeared; it was rather that they had gone into hiding because they believed her analyst hated children. I asked her where the boys had hidden themselves. She answered that they had hidden in her stomach. She had suffered for many years with difficult gastrointestinal symptoms.

I telephoned her analyst and advised him to speak to her about the fact that "the boys" believed he hated children. He tried to raise the issue with the patient, but was unable to avoid giving her the impression that he still hated children. He told her he wanted to know where she had gotten such a strange and incorrect notion. Their so-called treatment ended at this point. I knew this analyst well, and the boys were right in thinking that he hated children. The child he hated most of all, however, was the one he carried within himself. It was the traumatized child he had once been, whose painful experiences had been wholly disavowed. He was a very grown-up person, too much so, a highly cultured gentle-man who prided himself on his maturity and sophistication. If an analyst is not on friendly terms with the child within, there is no chance for there to be successful clinical work with patients such as the one I am describing. The world of ancient trauma simply cannot manifest itself, and if there are alters that have begun to crystallize, they will vanish in the face of the analyst's intolerance and hatred. An analyst who can bear his or her own childhood feelings, by contrast, will tend to respond maternally to any signs of such experiences in a patient, and the stage is then set for the coming forth of the trauma. Boys long forgotten come out of hid-ing, and the memories they hold have a chance to be more fully remembered and disclosed.

Having terminated her therapy, the patient began to see me instead. Her analyst felt I had engaged in unethical conduct by stealing his patient. I do not believe it is possible to steal anyone's patient, since patients are not possessions, but his attitude made the new treatment she and I were undertaking more stressful than it needed to be. It worked out pretty well nevertheless. The horrors of her early life were more completely explored, the boys were able to leave their hiding place and be recognized, and eventually, after many years, there were signs of a more complete wholeness than had been possible before.

At a certain point, she ceased to speak of boys, or of the little girls who were also included among the five alters that I met in this case. I did not ask where they had gone, knowing that they were not in hiding but rather that some important growth process was taking place. Finally, the patient developed a love for gardening. She planted an enclosed, beautiful flower garden arranged in a pentagon, where five different kinds of flowers would bloom simultaneously. It was implicit that the five areas of flowers corresponded to the five alters, and that the planting, nurturing, and enclosing of the garden enacted aspects of the coming together of the previously separated parts of herself. She and I never discussed this, however. Sometimes silence can be a fine and golden thing.

Am I arguing that the phenomena of dissociation are embedded in what is sometimes called an intersubjective field? Yes, as is all psychopathology, of every form and degree. People are what they are, feel what they feel, and do what they do in part because of how they have been and are being responded to by others. This is the human condition, for better and for worse. Dissociation itself can only occur in certain kinds of contexts, generally ones that deny a child the opportunity for his or her feelings to be recognized and validated in any way. A dissociative patient lives in a relational world that contains no room for the events that have vanished from recall. If any sign of the disappeared history shows itself, the child encounters reactions of incomprehension, hostility, and/or agonizing pain. Sometimes the child is marginalized or even excommunicated from the family. Once the space for those events materializes, on the other hand, perhaps in the patient finding someone to listen who can be a mother, they begin to reappear, along with the children to whom they happened. Eventually it all comes together and is really not all that complicated.

Examples are abundantly available to any clinician who works in this area. One that comes to mind concerns a 30-year-old woman who, as a child, had been horrifically abused by her grandfather. He had repeatedly raped and tortured her from when she was 4 years old until she was 11 or 12. All memory of the events had vanished as she grew into adulthood, the family system as a whole being one of consistent denial. At the age of 28, however, she began to have conversations with one of her cousins, a woman who, like herself, had been repeatedly attacked by the grandfather. The cousin was in treatment with a colleague for whom I served as the consultant. In the dialogue between the two of them, fragments of the lost memories began to reappear. The grandfather was an iconic figure in the family, revered and honored by all. Although his demonic side had victimized a number of family members, this was erased from the family system's conscious history. Finally the grandfather died and a great funeral and memorial service took place, an occasion for mourning the loss but also celebrating what everyone saw and needed to see as the greatness of his life. The woman I am speaking of chose this opportunity to break the silence, as she stood before the mourners and tried to give an account of how her grandfather had raped and tormented her. She bravely, or foolishly, was insisting that this was an occasion on which the truth could no longer be buried. Before the first sentences escaped her mouth, however, her brothers and uncles rushed up to her and carried her out of the meeting hall, throwing her into the street. She was told that what she had tried to do was unforgivable and that she was crazy.

She killed herself shortly after this incident. I think this was her way of trying to raise the stakes with her family, by staging an event, as she probably imagined it, so dramatic that they could not deny it. Sometimes the truth is much more important to a person than even life itself. This story is very sad and very depressing, though, because her plan did not work out at all. The family looked at her suicide and saw it as a confirmation that she was crazy. Denial systems such as this one cannot be broken down by direct confrontations with the truth. A space for that truth first has to be created.

Was there a way to have averted this death? I could do nothing: I was assisting in the treatment of her cousin, not her, and only found out about the whole story after the suicide. The patient about whose therapy I was consulting, by the way, equally a victim of the grandfather, was a multiple showing eight alters. The work with her continued for a great many years, and eventually a unifying wholeness gradually appeared. It was a serious battle, however, to keep her alive through most of this process.

Let us now return to a discussion of the subjective event of trauma itself, and the challenges we face as psychoanalytic therapists working with patients whose lives include such experiences. Is it the case that some things that may occur are simply, plainly just "too much"? Are there events that transpire in human lives that cannot be faced, that are, because of their magnitude, literally impossible to integrate into our sense of who we are? And if there are, then what do we do as clinicians in the face of these circumstances?

There are certainly events that feel unbearable. But are there things that happen which are literally beyond anyone's capacity to deal with? I don't see how one could answer a question such as this. I spoke to someone recently who told me he felt Mt. Everest had fallen upon him. The specific context was the eruption of long-dissociated pain relating to the deaths of his parents and a number of siblings and cousins when he was a boy. This person had had an earlier psychiatric consultation, and antidepressants had been recommended by the doctor he spoke to. He was so flooded that the psychiatrist deemed it advisable to contain and reduce the intensity of his suffering with a drug. I agree it is tough to manage Mr. Everest falling on oneself. But I would ask: What if Mt. Everest did fall on a person? What if the experience of the catastrophic pain is in exact proportion to the magnitude of the disaster that did indeed occur? Someone who has lost both parents and other family members during his childhood may well feel his entire world was coming to an end. Instead of taking measures to limit the pain being felt, I would try to empathize with the magnitude of the loss, to stay with the intensity of whatever the experience was.

If the experience is one that is impossible to bear, then that is what one stays with, the very impossibility of the unbearable pain. If one somehow becomes lost in the concreteness of it all, and perhaps agrees the person faces something impossible to withstand, then the only solution is to numb the pain with medications or alcohol, or maybe it would come up that suicide would be very effective as well. Such literality takes us nowhere we want to go. We need to resist the literalizing impulse and stay with the feeling that is present in the moment. If that feeling is one of Mt. Everest crashing down on one's head, so be it. In this story I would understand the patient's use of the metaphor of Mt. Everest as his way of trying to express the experience of his whole world having been crushed and destroyed. Maybe this is exactly what one could say to him.

It is unlikely that such a response would reduce the person's pain, but that is not a goal worth pursuing. A more meaningful goal would be to let the suffering be expressed, to allow the emotional truth of a life finally to have a chance to be put into words and images. A space is then being created for that pain that has not existed before. It might even be that the person's agony would increase in consequence of the sort of discussion I am suggesting, but he or she would then be more in the truth.

There is nothing wrong with wanting to reduce another person's pain, and one always hopes someone can find ways of living that are satisfying rather than full of suffering. A problem arises, though, when the analyst has a driving need to alleviate pain, when he or she cannot tolerate what may be a natural experience by the patient of intense negative affect. The reason so many psychotherapists are compelled to reduce their patients' pain has to do with the lives of the therapists themselves, with the family constellations in their histories that set them on a path toward their careers. It is almost always the same story: A sensitive child is enlisted by a parent to provide the emotionally sustaining, soothing nurturance that was missing in the parent's own developmental background. This is what Alice Miller called *The Drama of the Gifted Child* (1982). The original title of that book was *Prisoners of Childhood* (1979), which was much better. The analyst is captive to his mother and/or father, in the sense that he or she, unconsciously, is always drawn to alleviating the parents' (and patients') pain, and the grip of this mission is an imprisoning death camp for the analyst's soul. If the child, fated to become a psychotherapist later in life, breaks away from the role of soothing and otherwise supporting the parent, he or she catapults that parent into an agony state and is attacked and/or emotionally abandoned. This theme then plays out in the psychotherapy practice, where the real power of analysis—to address the truth of a life—becomes subverted by the ancient agenda of relieving parental pain. All kinds of strange collusions and evasions then begin to structure the analytic dialogue, defeating its potential to achieve its most important goals.

THE CHALLENGE OF UNDERSTANDING EXTREME TRAUMA

What are the greatest challenges facing our field in the area of the understanding and treatment of survivors of extreme trauma? These would be issues pertaining to the heart of the trauma experience and to what can and cannot be achieved in a psychotherapy process. They include the dream of purifying the soul of the effects of trauma, the freezing of time as a consequence of trauma, and the infinite isolation and loneliness created by trauma.

The term *trauma recovery*, if one thinks about it, is almost an oxymoron. Trauma, as I use the term anyway, is not just a terribly painful or shocking occurrence in a person's life; it is an event or series of events that is too much to bear, too much to take in as even having happened. The idea of recovery is about getting over something. I think there is no getting over real trauma. This sounds like a message of hopelessness, but it is not. Belief in the possibility of "recovery" from trauma, understood as a nullifying of the devastation, is a form of denial. Many analysts, and especially those that are animated by an unconscious goal of nurturing and healing a wounded parent, cannot understand this. Their commitment is to radical healing, a transformation that undoes the traumatic wound once and for all. Such clinicians encourage their patients' dreams that their terrible life histories can be transformed and purified, that the pain can be permanently removed and supplanted by a healing experience of joy and love. Such expectations are inevitably dashed, as the enduring reality of the traumatic injury continues to haunt the person's existence. There is no pot of gold at the end of the road of the psychotherapy of trauma. Under the best of conditions, what one does find there is a release from captivity, an increased wholeness, and also an abiding sense of sadness.

The traumatic events we are speaking of will affect the person down to the moment of his or her last breath. There is, however, hope for the person, for his or her life and future. Indeed, generally there is profound hope, and I would always seek to communicate a sense of that as someone is beginning to bear the unbearable and say the unsayable. But that future for which one can and should hope is not to be one free of the pain of the past; it will be a future that contains that pain, one that includes the events that formerly could not find a home anywhere. It will be a future of wholeness. This means that the individual becomes wholly present, and is no longer having to pour effort into being someone various things did not happen to. Good things flow from such a transformation, but the erasure of trauma is not one of them.

It is generally very difficult for a survivor of significant trauma to accept that there will be no purification, for such situations usually include all manner of curative fantasies that carry the hope of undoing the injuries of a traumatic past. Sometimes those fantasies are the only thing that has helped the person avert a suicide, so the realization of the irreversibility of trauma is fraught with danger. The role of the analyst is to work, in concert with the patient, to establish a setting that will come to include the unbearable and unsayable. The patient will fall, sometimes devastatingly, into despair in the course of this process, feeling there is no hope for survival at all. At such times the analyst must connect to that despair and reflect his or her developing understanding of its original and contemporary emotional contexts. In this way, he or she contradicts the patient's expectation that there is no place for the suffering that is felt, and a new context gradually comes into being wherein the unbearable can begin to be borne and the unsayable can begin to be said. This is the pathway toward wholeness, and it can be a very long one.

After a number of years of analytic work, a 25-year-old patient told me she had begun to remember having been sexually assaulted by her father as a small girl. The memories began slowly, with faint impressions of something bad having happened, something terrible that her father did. She begged me to tell her it was a matter of sick fabrications on her part, false memories, but I was unable to comply. Then the recall accelerated. There was a nightmare that occurred at the time, symbolizing the eruption of a long-buried history. In the dream, the patient was walking along a country road and encountered an outhouse. She opened the door and looked down into the toilet. She saw dark foaming liquid swirling about, going around and around. Then the motion of the liquid intensified and its level began to rise. Gurgling, foaming, it finally spewed forth violently in an explosive geyser. A torrent of dark memories afflicted her, including dozens of times in her early life when her father had come to her in the night and forced himself upon her sexually. She could not bear the recollections. "I can't live with this. It will kill me. I will kill myself. I have been killed. I am already dead so I want to be dead."

She was telling me life had become unlivable in consequence of the remembering, and so this is what I sought to stay with. She did not believe there could be any human understanding of what she had been through. It was her conviction, like that of every abuse victim I have ever known, that she was irredeemably bad, and by virtue of that badness, no one would respond to her suffering with anything except revulsion and hatred. That is a core aspect of the battle: to defeat such expectations. She and I talked to each other for 30 years.

She eventually did well; she became an exceptionally creative person, developed close friendships, married and raised two beautiful sons. She did not "recover," in the sense of erasing the pain of her childhood history. The incest imposed on her remained an enduring source of pain. She did, however, remember her whole history, and although it continued to be a source of suffering for her, she was not captive to it and did not repeat it. Abuse histories that are not remembered are always repeated upon the next generation or its surrogates; histories that are emotionally recalled, in contrast, are transformed into dangers one protects the next generation from.

My patient's father was still alive through the long course of her therapy, and one might wonder what happened between the two of them as she dealt with the tragedy of her early life. She was always polite with him outwardly, but she remained painfully aware that he had committed unforgivable crimes against her. I was actually present at a conversation between my patient and her aging father in which he said he was sorry about what had happened and begged her to forgive him. This talk occurred several decades after the original assaults. The father's request, passionately presented, was itself another crime committed against my patient, and it caused her great pain at the time. He seemed to be implying that if only she could accept his heart-felt apology, they could all move on and the terrible events of the past could be left behind. In other words, they could all recover. Such an idea is preposterous because there is no moving on from such crimes. There is, however, a freeing of a person from captivity, and such emancipation requires a journey into the truth of what has transpired. Nothing else will do. It would have helped my patient if her father could have said he knew what he had done was unforgivable, but he was unable to make such a statement. People capable of committing horrific crimes against children are generally unable to assume the human responsibility one would like to see.

The patient died from a cardiac infarction, suffered at age 56. It was very sudden and very sad. She did, however, get to see her sons grow up and led a very good life. She did not feel she had "recovered" from the traumas of her early years, nor should she have. She knew the truth of her own history and was able to do beautiful things with that knowledge. If more people had an equal level of self-understanding and awareness, this world would be a better place.

Consider now the second issue I raised pertaining to the challenges of psychotherapeutic work with the survivors of trauma: the "freezing of time." Time comes to a stop for a person subjected to extreme trauma, even as time continues to pass for that very same person in other respects. It is hard for a great many people to understand how this could be the case. It happens because something is impossible to go on with. I will provide a story in illustration.

A long time ago I met a woman whose husband had been killed by a drunk driver one afternoon, while he was on an errand for his family to pick up Italian bread for a spaghetti dinner. The tragedy had taken place many years before I met this person. She told me about all manner of difficulties in her life, and at the end of our discussion added that she never thought about her husband. I expressed amazement at this, and she responded:

> Well, never, except for in my dreams. I have the same dream about him every night. I dream every night that I am sitting at my kitchen table and my husband walks in with a loaf of bread. I have no idea why I should have such a dream. Do you think dreams mean anything?

Time stopped for this woman on the day of her husband's death. She had been sitting at her kitchen table, waiting for him to return with the Italian bread so the family could have its dinner. Eventually a policeman came and informed her that her husband had been killed. Her repeating dream shows that she was still sitting at that kitchen table, always waiting for her husband to return. Time had ceased to flow, and although in one respect clocks kept ticking and years kept passing, in another respect they did not. And strangely, she seemed not to know that a freezing of time had taken place. When I remarked about the apparent significance of her dreams, I thought I saw tears begin to form in her eyes. But then they receded.

Even sadder than what happened to her, however, was what she told me about the fate of her daughter, 12 years old at the time of the husband's awful death. The girl had loved her father above all others in heaven and on earth. She showed no disturbance in her life in consequence of the tragedy; if anything, her level of functioning seemed to rise over the course of the next years. She became a straight-A student in school, participated very actively in sports and social life, and eventually went on to an excellent college with full scholarship support. After graduating with a degree in architecture (her father had been in the construction industry), and looking toward a very bright professional future, she met a young man and fell in love. They decided to marry. Everything in her life seemed to be coming up roses. The disaster occurred when she and her young man announced their engagement and set a wedding date. She collapsed into a profound, unexplained depression. Suddenly she refused to get out of bed in the morning, saying she was paralyzed. "I feel there is something horribly heavy resting on top of me. Something is closing in on me. I can't live and I can't move and I can't breathe."

The mother called a local psychiatrist to get help for her daughter's sudden deterioration. She was referred to a medical group in a nearby university that was investigating and treating depressions in young adults having a sudden onset without identifiable precipitants. These doctors thought they had identified a distinct mental illness that had not been recognized in psychiatry up to that time. They called it "acute endogenous depression of young adulthood." Their idea was that this illness was organic in origin, related to subtle neurochemical changes in the brain, and they hoped to infer the nature of these changes by studying the effects of various experimental cocktails of drugs on the depressions in their patients. The young woman became their guinea pig. Great numbers of drugs and combinations of them were tried on her in the ensuing period, with mixed and unreliable results. She would briefly improve from the most severe extremes of her so-called depression, but then fall back into it and once again become unable to function.

I asked the mother if she had considered the possibility that her daughter's unexplained depression might be related to her father's sudden death that had taken place 10 years before. I added that, since there had been no signs of emotional disturbance during the interim, it was conceivable that the child's grief had been buried. The experience of the traumatic shock of the father's having been killed and then the pain of the mourning seemed nowhere evident in her history, and so I suggested she had saved these reactions up and now was being flooded by them. I added that her experience of a heavy weight on top of her might reflect an identification with her father, whom she was picturing as being crushed under 6 feet of earth. The feelings of being closed in and unable to breathe equally could be her way of being with him within the coffin, in his state of death, not moving, not breathing. Here too one sees an arrest in the passage of time, a resistance against moving forward in life, to building and embracing a meaningful future and a family of her own. Such progressive developments, in the context of this young woman's life, would mean departing forever from her beloved father and leaving him permanently behind. Inasmuch as he had been the center of this woman's life and his loss could not be grieved, this was not possible for her.

I urged the mother to seek some sort of psychological help for her daughter, focused on the buried grief and the factors interfering with it. To my surprise, she rejected this advice and said she and her daughter both had faith in the biological psychiatrists. A sick feeling came over me at this point, and later that day I became violently ill. I do not ordinarily express my emotional reactions to distressing events in bodily reactions, but in this instance I was tremendously disturbed by the mother's refusals to even consider the possibility in her daughter's life of an arrested grief reaction. I did not speak to the woman again for many years. Almost two decades later, she developed a metastatic cancer, and returned to me for a single consultation. This presented an opportunity to ask about what had happened to her daughter. It was so sad. For all the years that had elapsed in the meantime, the drug trials continued; the daughter had been in and out of psychiatric hospitals, and her planned marriage and career—and really her whole life—lay in ruins. Her fiancée had left her; she never worked as an architect; and she had become massively obese as her weight ballooned up as an apparent effect of the many drugs she continued to take.

Why could the daughter not grieve the loss of her father? Granted, his violent death was a trauma and a terrible shock, and yet, still and all, other daughters manage to come to terms with such tragedies without destroying themselves and their lives. The story, if I have understood it correctly, is of a family in which there was no possibility of mourning the loss, and the daughter's so-called illness—her "acute endogenous depression of young adulthood," as her doctors wished to think of it—was her way of preserving contact through an identification with her father in his state of death. The mother also maintained a tie to her lost husband, as reflected in her repeating dreams of him returning home with the Italian bread. The mother refused to consider the possibility that her daughter was captive to an arrested grief reaction. I think for her to have accepted this would have required her to confront her own mourning, something her dreams suggest was not possible for her as well. There must have been reasons for why no mourning could occur.

Let us imagine that something went terribly wrong early in her life between the daughter and her mother, something that meant no real relationship between the two of them could continue. There were some signs in the mother of an enveloping narcissism, and she may have been one of those who invites her child on a journey from which there will be no return. Imagine further that the tie to the father then became the foundation of the daughter's life and being. To grieve the loss of the father then would have meant giving up the one in relation to whom her very existence as a person was sustained. Under such circumstances, mourning cannot occur, and the lost parent remains as an enduring presence to the surviving child. I would assume the father's existence was maintained somehow throughout her adolescence, perhaps in part by her molding herself into a duplicate of him in a female body. Whatever the path of keeping him alive was, it could not continue once she entered into her own anticipated marriage. Perhaps the wedding plans triggered her collapse, when she began to think about the part of the ceremony in which the father gives away the bride. Her identity as a person being contingent on feeling connected to him, a more dramatic symbol of that closeness then broke into being: her deathlike depression. The clinical work in a case such as this consists in the exploration of the tie to the lost parent, of its foundational function in sustaining the child's being, and of all the circumstances and events that played a role in magnifying that function. One hopes such an exploring will set the stage for a more productive form of mourning that will not cost the young woman her life. No attempt along this line was made.

And now, the mother: Evidently, she too held the husband at the center of her existence, and she continued her relationship with him in her dreams, forever awaiting his return home from the trip to the store to buy bread. It could be that her story is the mirror of her daughter's: She too had been exclusively tied to her own father and dependent on him for her sense of being. Maybe her husband inherited this function in her life, and as a consequence there was no possibility of accepting the death and mourning the loss. I never came to know her well enough to be sure that this was the general story, but I have known many such cases over the years.

The tragedy in this family, involving both mother and daughter in an arrest in the passage of time, was associated with a death, but extreme traumas of other kinds also freeze time. The reason is not complicated: It is always a matter of something happening that one simply cannot make into a part of one's history. It then remains in an eternal now, perhaps hidden away in a persistent amnesia.

THE CASE OF JEANNE

The story about the woman and her daughter is tragic, but is mostly conjecture. I shall now give another account illustrating the freezing of time more directly. It involves my first clinical case of so-called dissociative identity disorder, a woman whom I call Jeanne. The events to be described happened 40 years ago. I had been working with this person, then 24, for perhaps 18 months. She was suffering with some serious depressions that came and went, and my understanding of her at the time centered around a lasting loneliness she seemed to feel that traced back into her childhood. Her early years were filled with abuse in which she became the target of physical violence from both her mother and her father. She also witnessed many savage beatings inflicted on her younger brother. Part of her reaction to this challenging family context was to become absorbed in an imaginary world populated by the ghosts of relatives who had died before she was born. These were people who had lived in Eastern Europe and were buried there. She repeatedly traveled to their gravesites, in an imagined out-of-body state, and immersed herself in positive, loving contacts with the dead that contrasted with the deprivation and violence she experienced in her home at the hands of the living. Although I saw clearly the extremity of the child abuse that had taken place, it did not occur to me that she might be a multiple until one night something happened that indicated it unequivocally. I received a telephone call from someone speaking in a high, falsetto voice. I asked her who she was, not recognizing that it was this patient. The answer coming back was: "This is little girl...I am 4 years old...She—doesn't know about me...I want to tell you where I come from."

I realized at this point that this was my patient, and that I was speaking to an alter. I asked her to go ahead and tell me where she came from.

> I am in a room full of grownups. It's a party. A door opens and someone comes in carrying a silver platter. There is a baby boy on

the platter. They put it down on the table. Then a tall man with a beard comes in. He is carrying a knife. He goes over to the baby and takes the knife and cuts the baby's penis. The baby screams and blood spurts out of his penis. All the people in the room clap and hug each other and smile and cheer. I don't want to be like these people. They think it's fun to hurt babies. I don't ever want to grow up. I will never grow up.

Time froze for this little girl, and thenceforth she did not age, like Peter Pan, remaining just 4 years old, although chronologically the patient was 24. She—the 4-year-old—had lived in the meantime in a secret world, but was now coming out to make contact with me.

The bris that had taken place was held in her mind as an inexplicably joyful attack by grownups on the most vulnerable part of a defenseless infant's body. The 4-year-old turned out to be one of six alters in all. Each of the patient's various personalities was associated with a specific moment at which events occurred that were impossible to integrate. Her history therefore was not a linear unfolding over the course of the years; it was, rather, a discontinuous sequence in which the different unbearable moments giving rise to the alters remained embedded within a fractured, traumatic temporality (Stolorow, 2011).

The psychotherapy for Jeanne consisted in a long journey of reliving and remembering. Each of the pivotal traumas reappeared in the therapeutic dialogue, often involving extended periods in which she confused me with the perpetrators of the crimes that had been committed against her. There were suicide attempts, physical attacks on me, and repeated episodes of cutting and other dangerous abuse of herself in my presence. The events of her shattered history thus came alive again, and I can say that bearing with this extended process of resurrecting a frozen past— it required almost 4 years—was among the most stressful and difficult clinical experiences I have ever had to endure.

After what felt like endless tears and blood, the central traumatic moments of her history began to transform into memories of terrible events and lost their previous tendency to be passionately reenacted and relived as present realities. In the course of this arduous process, the alters, previously having been very distinct and separate from one another, slowly lost their distinctiveness, began to resemble one another, and finally integrated into a single personal identity. The unification was announced with great drama, when she one day cried out: "We are Me! I am one now—we voted last night, and all agree!"

Then she cleared off the desk in my office and threw down 12 small slips of paper on its surface. On six of the slips were written the names of the six alters. On the other slips were short descriptions of the traumatic incidents that originally produced the dissociations. She asked me in a challenging tone if I thought I could match which description went with which alter. Before allowing me to make the pairings, she pushed me out of the way and undertook the task herself. She arranged two closely juxtaposed columns on the desktop: one displaying the names of the six personalities in the temporal sequence of their appearance in her life, and the other the disastrous events with which the alters were variously associated. The enactment concretized the transformation of her shattered history into a unified, historically continuous structure, and from this moment on in her life she was whole. I was able to follow the development of her life over the next four decades, and the unity she had achieved remained evident throughout.

The case of Jeanne is also relevant to the theme of infinite isolation. The little-girl part of her lived in a place of everlasting solitude, cut off from all communication with living human beings. Her only contacts were with ghostly entities she saw in the out-of-body journeys to the graves of distant relatives in Europe. The loneliness of the trauma victim is of the most extreme kind that one can imagine: It has as its essential feature that it is felt as absolute, never to be relieved. The loneliness is cosmic, rather than terrestrial. It extends throughout the universe and seems, to the person suffering it, to be eternal. It is not conceivable that it can ever be addressed, diminished, soothed, escaped. It is damnation.

This experience of being forever in darkness may become more compellingly real than any other. We must understand how such a feeling can lead someone to very extreme acts, sometimes acts of great destructiveness. I was asked to consult on a most terrible case some years ago—that of a man who had taken it upon himself to murder a number of little girls. He had killed himself after ending the lives of the children, by shooting them. The question I was asked to address by one of the authorities involved was the motive of the killer. His crime seemed not to be anything anyone could understand. Why kill innocent little girls? I offered a theory, based on a few details of the case, but my thinking was ignored by those investigating the incident. My theory was that he had attacked and killed out of a sense of eternal isolation.

There is a principle that applies to pretty much all these atrocities. One reads about serial murders of children, but there is always one additional death that does not appear in the news reports: the original murder of the killer's own soul, generally a crime that has taken place long, long before. The serial killing of children is a restaging of an original murder, spiritual rather than physical in nature. It is history being reenacted, but with the original victim now recast as the active controlling agent in the drama. The powerlessness of the early victimization is thereby replaced by godlike control over the life and death of the other. Sometimes this reversal is enhanced by becoming suffused with sexual intensity.

There were a few facts in the case that directed me to the theme of loneliness. This man had access to children of both sexes, but chose to kill girls, not boys. Secondly, he had a history of chronic anguish over the loss of his own firstborn child, a girl, who died shortly after her birth. He agonized over a period of many years about the death of this child, saying he was unable to accept the fact that her life had ended before it had a real chance even to begin. His loss of her seemed to be more important to him than his later children, all boys, who survived. This initial baby girl was some-one the man could not have come to meaningfully know—she died upon being born—and yet she seems to have been the most important person in the world to him.

I asked the question: What is going on here? An idea then came to me: His firstborn child must have been a symbol of this man's own original innocence. She was his inner, essential child-self, reincarnated, only to die immediately having been given a second chance at life. He must have himself been killed as a small boy by something that happened in his family, in a murder of the soul. Perhaps that soul was that of a girl from the beginning. Such a thing comes about when there are forces in a child's world that lead to an active disidentification with those of one's own gender. The overall circumstances, suggested by details about his fantasies and obsessions, almost certainly involved a series of traumatic sexual attacks or their equivalents against him.

The sexually violated child is catapulted into a realm of suffering that feels, to that child, at an infinite remove from human contact. It is a searing, emotionally disfiguring sort of thing that leaves one believing life has ended and one has been cast into the darkness. This is where the loneliness sets in, for the experience is so extreme that it is unimaginable that anyone will be able or willing even to approach it. This is what generally causes the wall of silence to appear in childhood sexual abuse. And yet, such an exclusion from participation in the community of others is itself not bearable for a person. A driving desire arises to close that infinite gap, to somehow draw the world of the light and the world of the darkness back together again.

My idea was that this man's core life experience had originally been the violation and utter destruction of his own childhood soul—the most precious of all precious things to a little boy or little girl. He had lived, thenceforth, in a damnation state, alone with this terrible emotional reality. By killing a series of female children, the most treasured things in the lives of their families, I think he imagined a drawing down into the darkness of the grieving parents, maybe also of the girls themselves, and therefore a relieving of the infinite loneliness by which he had been afflicted. The man wanted some companions in the cavern, and he killed in order to get them.

Was there anything that could have been done for this man, before he committed the murders? Or would this be a case that was hopeless, the traumas and injuries being too deep and beyond the reach of meaningful human response? We will never know. My thought was that it was *his* experience that he was beyond the reach of the human world, and that his terrible actions were direct responses to that felt reality. It is at least imaginable that a different outcome could have been achieved if there had been someone deeply involved with this man who was trying to find him. Maybe that person could have communicated that he understood the drive to kill defenseless children as borne out of the need to make others feel as he did, so that someone else would know something comparable to the agony of his losses. Maybe it could be said that if he carried out the terrible crimes, then the shattered families would know what it means when everything you believe in and hope for is murdered.

The consequences of the traumatic solitude experience can be deadly; among the destructive things that can happen, however, suicide is much more common than becoming a killer of others. But sometimes the opposite altogether occurs, especially when the human environment of the trauma survivor is a favorable one. It can be that great creative expressions flow out of experiences of trauma, expressions that themselves also relate to the solitude of the darkness.

Almost every truly creative act I have ever studied might constitute an example. To take just one, consider the great poet Maya Angelou, author of *I Know Why the Caged Bird Sings* (1969). During her middle childhood years, she was repeatedly molested and then violently raped by her mother's boyfriend. He told her he would kill her beloved older brother if she spoke about the sexual attacks. She tried to hide what had occurred, but it was discovered by her family and finally the truth came out. Although the boyfriend was arrested and charged, he was murdered, possibly by Maya Angelou's own relatives, before he could serve his prison time for his crimes. For the next years, she remained almost completely mute, locked in a cage of silence. It is understandable that she stopped talking, in view of the boyfriend's threats against her brother and also the fact that he was murdered, by being beaten to death. But even in the absence of such threats and violence, a wall of silence materializes. Finally, helped by her brother, her grandmother, and a teacher who encouraged her interest in literature, she began to speak again. And then later, after a long struggle which included a near-suicide, the caged bird began to sing, and sing, and sing. I listened to her at Bill Clinton's 1993 inauguration, reading a gorgeous poem entitled, "On the Pulse of Morning." Drawing on her own lonely journey into the darkness, she has given hope to all those who are lost that they might be found.

The traumatic isolation experience is one of estrangement from all things human. That is the challenge for the clinician: to extend the reach of his or her empathy to precisely this subjective state, drawing the feeling of having been cast into the darkness back into the community of others as something humanly recognizable. It is the miracle of psychotherapy that it can sometimes render the unbearable bearable and the unsayable sayable. This occurs, however, not by diminishing the pain one encounters in the world of the trauma survivor, which is impossible, but by including that pain within the circle of human understanding.

6

The Tragedy of Self-Destruction

They leave all hope behind who enter there:
One certitude while sane they cannot leave,
One anodyne for torture and despair;
The certainty of death.

James Thomson
The City of Dreadful Night

Human beings are the only animals known that commit suicide. Why do they do this? I carry significant trauma from a number of friends, teachers, and patients who have chosen to end their lives. I will begin by describing one of these.

Professor Jack C. was a faculty member in the psychology department at the University of Arizona during the period in the early 1960s when I was a student there. He was my major advisor; I took three courses from him, and in my final year at Arizona he became my friend. A year and a half after I graduated, he went out into the desert, poured a can of gasoline on himself, and lit himself ablaze and died horribly.

I have been haunted by this death for almost half a century, always wondering about its cause and its meaning. This chapter, beginning with some conjectures about my teacher's tragic fate, branches out into a wide-ranging discussion of the act of self-destruction.

SEIZING POWER IN THE CAVERN OF DESPAIR

The terrible death of Dr. C. took place shortly after I completed my undergraduate studies. I was as close to him as I had been to any teacher up until that time, and the shock and sadness I felt upon learning of his death have never left me.

Dr. C. was a young man, perhaps 36 years old, who specialized in mathematical learning theory. He was building a career around conducting experimental tests of the theoretical frameworks of Clark Hull and Kenneth Spence. One of my first publications was an article coauthored with him and two others presenting such an experiment: "The Overtraining Reversal Effect under Two Types of Discrimination" (Tempone, Capehart, Atwood, & Golding, 1966).

The theories of Hull and Spence were attempts to construct a Newtonian physics of animal and human behavior. Their thinking was the antithesis of the soft humanistic and existential traditions that are so dear to my heart, and so one might wonder what I was doing working on such a project. It is a sad story. Psychology at my university was in the grip of behaviorists. Professor C., a gentle man, was the one I got along with best. I found that studying and working with mathematical learning theory was a kind of game one could play, not even as complicated as chess, and so it was my adaptation to an academic environment that for the most part was hostile to my deepest interests. I came to psychology through an earlier exposure to the works of Freud and especially Jung; to my dismay, I found another kind of psychology altogether being taught at my college, one that was inimical to psychoanalytic thinking.

I got along well with Professor C. I felt he liked and appreciated me quite a lot, and it was enjoyable, in a gamelike way, to do the experimentation and study the theories in which he specialized. I did not entirely compromise my values in joining my teacher's research program, in that I made no secret of the fact that my greatest interests were not in behaviorism but in the works of Freud and Jung. I used to walk around the department carrying one of the volumes of Jung's collected works with me. I was known there as "that weird Jungian guy."

Dr. C. knew of my interest in Jung, but had never spoken a word to me about it until just before my graduation. He called me at home and asked me to come to his office so that he could tell me something. I was extremely curious about what this was to be, and a little worried that he might be about to hit on me. I arrived, and he said:

> Come in and sit down, my friend. I have asked you to come by because I have a small confession to make. It concerns something I never talk to anyone about. I know you have had quite an interest in the teachings of Carl Gustav Jung. Well, it turns out, so have I. You may be aware that I live alone. Most evenings when I am ready to retire, I open my closet and bring out one of Jung's books. I have quite a library of his most important works. I light a candle, and then, in the soft light, immerse myself in his thought. I guessed you might like to know about this, but I must ask you to keep it to yourself.

He smiled sweetly after the little confession. I thanked him for revealing his secret love of Jung and promised to say nothing of it to anyone. Now that he is dead I don't feel I have to keep that promise. I found it amazing, and intensely pleasing, that I had gravitated to the one behaviorist who had a hidden interest in the very things that drew me into the field of psychology. It felt like a validating confirmation of my own thinking, as I struggled otherwise to survive intellectually in a wasteland of positivism and empiricism.

So the Newtonian psychologist was a closet Jungian, literally! I am not sure, as I think about this story now, that there wasn't an erotic undercurrent in Dr. C.'s overture to me, but nothing direct ever appeared. I see, however, something I was unable to appreciate then: There was a rift, like a deep canyon, right down the center of his personality. By day he was an arch-rationalist, wearing a white laboratory coat and performing quantitative analyses on animal and human behavior; by night he was a candle-burning Jungian mystic inhabiting a world of secrecy. It is kind of sad that only in his student, George Atwood, did he find someone who could know about and perhaps respect both sides—a person with whom he could therefore be a bit more whole. I could not at that time have understood the profundity of what he was doing in inviting me to the office chat. I was only 20 years old.

After the revelation of his secret, I thanked him and left. I never saw him again. About a year later I received a letter from a graduate student at Arizona, someone I had befriended during the years of my research under Dr. C. I still have that letter, and here are its exact words:

> George—I don't know if you heard, but something terrible happened to Jack C. He burned himself alive in the desert outside of town [Tucson, AZ]. No one understands it, but this much is known. He fell in love with one of our new graduate students in the clinical psychology program, and apparently decided she was his one true love of a lifetime, his soul mate. When he approached her, however, she rebuffed his advances and told him that she was not interested in a relationship with him. He left a note to her at the site where he incinerated himself. It said: "Dear Sarah—I may not have you in this life, but I know we will be together in the next!" Sarah herself, whom I've gotten to know a bit, is totally blown away.

After years of thought on the matter of this death, which otherwise just seems awful and incomprehensible, a few ideas have come to me regarding its meaning. Sarah was Dr. C.'s eternal soul mate, the woman who could complete his life and heal his fractured soul. What produces such an idealization—one that becomes more important than the preservation of life itself? We don't know, but I would picture a trauma of great power that occurred in the first two or at most three years of his life. Perhaps it was something similar to what happened to Jung (1961) as a very young child: a devastatingly long separation from his beloved mother. In Jung's case, the traumatic rupture of the tie to his mother contributed to a subsequent splitting of his selfhood into two distinct parts, what he came to call his No. 1 and No. 2

personalities. I think something parallel happened to my teacher when he was very young, an earthquake in his soul that left him divided into two parts. I picture one of these parts—rather like Jung's No. 1 personality—being logical, realistic, and oriented to the immediate external world. This would be the aspect of Jack C. that became a behaviorist, fitting itself into an academic psychology that was trying to construct itself on the model of the sciences of nature. The other aspect of my doomed professor, corresponding to Jung's No. 2 personality, was not grounded in immediate reality, perhaps considered itself to belong to another realm of being altogether, and contained the longing for a sense of connection tracing back to an experience of profound early loss. This was the part that would rise into prominence in the nightly rituals of lighting candles and retrieving Jung's writings from his closet.

Like my teacher, Jung was deeply affected when, as an adult, he met a woman who seemed to him to be his soul mate (Wehr, 2001). There are two important differences, though. One is that the woman Jung selected was responsive to his advances and tried her best to take care of him. The other is that he was able to channel the emotional disturbance he underwent back into his intellectual work, for example in his formulation of the theory of the anima archetype. Dr. C. had neither the girl nor the theory, and—if I am right in my speculations—he was left with a disastrous repetition of his early-loss experiences. He reached for a magical relationship with Sarah, his anima figure, in the hope of mending a broken self, soothing a loneliness that had afflicted him from an early age, and recovering a bond of all-encompassing maternal love. Her refusal to have anything to do with him cast him into the darkness and recapitulated his experiences of being unloved and abandoned. There must have been unbearable pain. People tend to kill themselves in such situations.

It is notable that, in choosing death, Professor C. fought off his despair to a degree and held on to the dream of union with his beloved. Perhaps he thought that going out in a blaze of glory would inform Sarah of the depth of his passion, and she would be inspired to find him in the life that is to come. He and she could then consummate their shared destiny against a background of everlasting life. A little boy would find his mother again, and all that had been wrong could be set right. As I think about this man's life and death, my heart breaks.

The sadness brought on by Jack C.'s death deepened significantly a number of months later, when I learned that his colleague and friend, Vincent T. (also my teacher, and also a coauthor on my early publication) killed himself as well. However, I was never able to learn anything about this latter suicide, except that it was carried out with a handgun.

Would it have been possible to help Professor C.? We will obviously never know, but I think we should always be hopeful in the midst of such developments. It has been my experience that our hope in the face of a person's despair is often the primary thing that makes the difference. If I can imagine him encountering someone in a position to understand him—perhaps a George Atwood 30 years older—I can also picture him having an experience that could have helped him survive.

I have discussed what happened to my professor with a number of psychoanalysts over the years, and have often heard it said that he must have been in a rage against his beloved Sarah, and against the early parental figure for which she was the surrogate. The idea that the act of self-destruction is about rage against the faithless, abandoning other strikes me as based on a confusion. This notion originates of course in Freud's famous formulations in his essay, "Mourning and Melancholia" (1917). Suicide comes not from rage and hatred, in my experience, but from despair. My teacher did not burn himself up out of a deep desire to destroy his beloved. He did not have a wish to retaliate that became deflected onto himself. He killed himself because the prospect of a life without her was unbearably painful and offered no pathway to survival that he could see. I can believe that the student Sarah was deeply wounded by the death, but to say that this was its aim, at whatever level, is to confuse the result with the motive. If we look at the suicide note, it tells us he chose death in order to be with his soul mate, and one doesn't need to go beyond that.

I think of suicide as a kind of door that stands before us, a possibility available to every human being. It is there because we are aware of the existence of death, of its inevitability in any case, and we are free to make it occur as a volitional act. Anyone is capable of walking through that door; all that is needed is the right set of circumstances. When something unbearable is happening and no way can be seen to change it, suicide occurs. The worst has appeared, and there is no doorway out. But yet there is always just one: It has the word *Death* written on it. It is the doorway to self-destruction, chosen as an alternative to intolerable pain and helplessness. It is a seizing hold of power, in a cavern of despair.

THE CASE OF DAVID

I shall now tell a story of a suicide averted. A man I will call David asked for an appointment at the behest of his wife. He was a 30-year-old Ph.D. in computer science, working for a major corporation. He lived with his wife, and there were two stepchildren, from her previous marriage. I noted upon meeting him that he was very tall and remarkably thin. Asked what brought him to me, he answered that he had been having rage reactions in his home. If anyone—his wife, his stepchildren, even his pet dog and cat—approached him suddenly and intrusively, he would erupt with shouting and cursing. David's family had become frightened of him, and his wife insisted that he undergo counseling to help him control his temper. He told me he needed anger management treatments.

We spoke for close to an hour about the rage episodes, which had been growing more frequent and violent for some months. We also spoke briefly about his background. He was an only child in a Jewish family, one who showed stellar academic ability throughout his childhood. He had been an A-plus student always, with special talents in mathematics and science. David graduated early from high school and studied computer science at one of the top colleges in our nation. Receiving a Ph.D. at age 23, he had immediately gone to work at a major corporation and earned a very high salary. A few years later, he met a woman at his place of employment, and they married. She had had an earlier marriage and two children, and was several years older than he.

As our initial session drew to a close, I was puzzled, because although I could see his increasing distress and reactivity in his home, there was no reason for it in the information he provided. He seemed himself to be at a complete loss. I scheduled a second appointment for a few days later, and he rose to leave. Just before going out the door, however, he turned and said:

> Oh, there is just one thing—a question I wanted to ask. I have been thinking of tossing a coin later this evening. If it comes up heads, then I will live, for now. But if it turns up tails, I will kill myself. Do you think there is anything the matter with this idea?

I had a sensation of ice water flowing down my back as I listened to him speaking about this, because there was no doubt whatsoever that he was ready to end his life. Fortunately, I had 2 hours free on the other side of this first appointment, and I insisted he stay and talk with me further. I asked him how he could allow the outcome of a coin toss to determine whether his life continued. He said he did not care which way it came out, because his life had no value to him. Given that he was completely indifferent, it had seemed to be a good idea to let the random outcome of tossing a coin make the decision.

I told him that there had to be a reason why his life had no value to him, and we needed to understand what that was. We spoke for the full 2 hours, and it turned out that we were able to identify the source of his indifference. I will sum it up as follows: David did not care whether he lived or died because his life had never been his own in any case. He had developed, from an extremely early age, as the brilliant, successful child his father and especially his mother wanted and needed him to be. They regarded him as a gift from God, someone whose extraordinary achievements made them proud and confirmed the value of their lives. Similarly in his marriage, he was the faithful, devoted husband his wife expected, and he had also been the good stepfather her children looked to him to be. That is, until the rages appeared. He and I were able to say that something within him had begun to fight against the reign of compliance that had dominated his existence theretofore, and we were able to say as well that the pathway of our work together would be one of helping him claim his own life for himself. In the meantime, he agreed to refrain from tossing any coins. An immediate effect of this understanding was that his rages vanished, and they never returned.

I worked with him for 19 years, and every aspect of that work centered around his establishing a sense of personal control over his situation, building a life that he could experience as belonging to no one except for himself. His outer situation changed in the course of this work: He divorced his wife, quit his job, and became a highly successful independent contractor in information technologies. Inwardly, the transformation was also very profound. Approximately 10 years into our process, he suffered through a long period of intense, almost debilitating spells of death anxiety. David would awaken in the middle of the night, his heart pounding, with tremendous fears that he was having a fatal heart attack. It helped him for us to say that this fear of death was an emergent sign that his life had finally become something that was precious to him. I noticed also that he had begun to gain weight. For the first time, he said, he had begun to like the taste of food. All things considered, things worked out very well for him. But he was almost lost to this world right at the beginning.

One could ask what might have happened to David at the beginning of this story if he had tossed his coin and it came up heads. I would answer that he would have gone for two out of three, then three out of five. He was deadly serious about suicide. I have looked at a number of similar cases where the deed was accomplished. One reads about them now and then in the newspapers: A high school valedictorian, with everything to live for, hangs himself; a summa cum laude, voted most likely to succeed, jumps out a window. These are people who have lived for others and their lives have no value for them. The only genuine thing they have done is finally to say *no* to continuing the compliance. In a life based entirely on lies, the only authentic action possible is suicide.

Of course the opposite of this is also the case. Inasmuch as such young people have been denied the space they need to live authentically, self-destruction is a form of surrender to that negating world. In a life based entirely on lies, the ultimate act of compliance is suicide.

THE CASE OF LARRY

Here is another very sad story, concerning the death of a young man who was my best friend in the late 1960s. His name was Larry, and he was a fellow clinical psychologist at the hospital where I did my postdoctoral training. He was what they call an "ABD," meaning a psychologist who completed all his education but his dissertation. He was a classic procrastinator, and his career as a clinician was significantly held back by his inability to complete the empirical studies he had tried to plan. They were studies attempting to interrelate various subscales of the Minnesota Multiphasic Personality Inventory (MMPI) (McKinley & Hathaway, 1944) in somewhat unusual ways. Anyway, he shot himself in the head with a rifle almost 40 years ago, but a day does not pass that I do not think of him.

Larry's death was emotionally devastating because it came at a time when he was the person in my life that I felt closest to. Various features of his situation, looked at in retrospect, were signs of something terribly wrong, but neither I nor anyone else understood his suffering. In the years and decades since, I have tried to make sense of the tragedy. Here are the conjectures that have arisen out of a long effort to interpret meaning in a disaster that otherwise floats before my mind in senseless absurdity.

I tried to help him on his unfinished doctoral thesis and so learned about the ideas he had hoped to pursue. He was studying how one could take the various scales of the MMPI two at a time, and correlate them with all the rest singly or in various combinations. The notion was that there might be interesting regularities, previously unseen patterns of interconnectedness, that could be demonstrated statistically. And then there was the further idea that these patterns, once found, might be indicators of previously unseen dimensions of psychopathology in general. It was all rather imprecise, very incompletely conceptualized; I found I was unable to assist him in making his project into something practical for completing his doctoral degree.

This study, looking back now, could never have eventuated in anything even remotely interesting, and my friend's procrastination may well have had to do with the fact that he saw his research was destined to come to nothing. The MMPI is a paper-and-pencil questionnaire that reduces psychopathology to a series of discrete traits that are then quantified according to how many statements in particular groups the person agrees with. Psychopathology does not exist as a set of quantifiable traits, and the construction of this instrument was therefore misguided from the outset. During my student years, I read through the test, and the individual items patients taking it are asked to mark true or false made me laugh. The one I remember today is: "I often have black tarry bowel movements." I do not have such bowel movements, at least not often, but if I did, I doubt I would want my psychologist to know about it. Why am I being asked about this? It's enough to make a person paranoid. The test is a joke, played on psychiatric patients and on American psychology, which has always been in love with anything that appears to quantify the mind. So I am thinking my friend Larry must have known all this, and even so he persisted with his ideas. Why did he do this?

The MMPI divides its items into groups supposedly measuring different psychopathological trends, like "depression," "paranoia," "schizophrenia," "psychopathic deviance," and so on. So Larry was looking at these traits, dimensions, or whatever we want to call them, and he imagined that there were hidden interconnections between them, subtle coherences he could perhaps tease out statistically. A fantasy underlies my poor friend's project: It may have been a symbol of an effort to synthesize a sense of his own coherence out of previously disparate elements. Perhaps he was a man who had not found his own identity and was expressing this quest, and his failure to fulfill it, by the strange, unfinished Ph.D. dissertation. Procrastination is a matter of not being able to complete the tasks that are undertaken. Perhaps the central task he could not complete was one of becoming himself. It is possible that the raw materials out of which Larry was trying to assemble something, as he experienced them, were just various trends of illness existing within him. It's as if he were saying: "Let me take all my failings, all the ways I am nothing more than a fragmented, sick bastard, and try to find some order and wholeness out of combining them together." He was a man whose self-esteem was beneath the basement. He also seems to have been someone who never fully arrived in this world.

Still, he was very smart and had what I experienced as a real sense of humor, with a pleasing cynical edge. We had many intellectual conversations about psychology and psychiatry, philosophy, history, economics, and politics. I will give just one example of the kind of thing he would say that appealed to me. One Sunday morning he came over for coffee, and our conversation turned to the methodological agendas of our shared discipline and their background in the philosophical doctrine known as positivism. The conventional definition of this position is given in the statement: "All true observation is external to the observer." I offered to Larry an alternative expression, self-canceling in its structure: "All those propositions not grounded in objective external data are to be cast into the flames!" He chuckled, and responded in a western-sounding drawl: "Ahhhh yes, positivism: the doctrine that flies up its own asshole."

He was obsessed with the economic state of the world, and often forecast the coming of a great depression that would make the collapse of 1929 look like a walk in the park. I don't recall that he had detailed knowledge of economic history, but I know his thinking was very left wing, and vaguely Marxist. It bothered me that he was so certain that financial doom was just around the corner, and I sometimes was afraid he was projecting his own anticipated personal catastrophe. What I was not able to see then was that the disaster he foresaw in the future was most likely a memory, cast forward in time, of a calamity from long ago. I derive this idea from Winnicott's (1974) famous essay on the fear of breakdown. I see now something terrible in my friend's childhood background: a trauma, or series of them, of massive proportions.

Larry hardly had a thing to say about his early life. He was an only child in a Jewish family, and he had only one memory from the first 6 or 7 years of his life. It was a visual/auditory recollection of his mother approaching him, closer and closer, moving her forefingers on both hands in repetitive circular motions, and making a buzzing sound, like a bumblebee. Just that: his mother approaching, and the sound of "zzzzzzzzzzzz." The feeling accompanying the image was one of fear.

The absence of conscious memories of the early years is probably a sign of extreme trauma, and of an accompanying dissociative reaction. When there is a single vivid memory image like the one of his mother, we are well advised to dwell with it and consider it to be a window into all that is otherwise hidden. It is a memory of impingement, intrusion, invasive action. I wonder if she was one of those fine mothers who consider it their duty to inflict repeated cleansing enemas, in the process violating the child's developing sense of bodily integrity and disrupting the establishment of personal identity and agency. The alarming sound of the buzzing bumblebee connotes something inescapable, painful, perhaps poisonous; the image contains the implication that there is absolutely no way out. I think this little boy became subject to his mother's madness, and that he dealt with the trauma by burying his feelings and emotionally distancing himself from her.

He never wanted to talk about his mother, and he did not have anything to say about his father either. Larry gave the strong impression that his father was somehow absent, physically and emotionally. I picture him as a boy turning to this absent father, or trying to. He would have had to do anything he could to survive his mother's madness, to please his dad, to make him proud. A crazy mother cannot do that much harm if there is an alternative in the family. I have the sense, though, that Larry could not find the paternal rescue.

Here is something that happened a few months before my friend killed himself. I learned of this in a letter from his girlfriend. These are her actual words:

> Larry told a story about a nightmarish bus ride he had from St. Louis to Kansas City. He said halfway through the trip, a big "redneck" stood up and began berating a young black man sitting in the back of the bus. He seemed to be in a drunken rage. The yelling and cursing continued for a few minutes and finally the redneck ordered the black guy off the bus. The driver stopped, and the man quietly departed. Larry did not protest and everyone else remained silent.

This was only the beginning. In the ensuing days and weeks, my friend became obsessed with the incident on the bus, experiencing a deepening shame at how he had just sat there quietly while a racist carried out an attack on an innocent man. Then it came to him: The whole scene had been staged by the Communist Party, to test the depth and sincerity of his moral convictions. Larry had failed the test, clearly, and now was rightly held in contempt among those behind the coming revolution. He had had his chance to stand up for the oppressed, and he had surrendered and was now in everlasting disgrace.

This dreamlike tale, especially with the delusional elaboration regarding the Communists, led me to questions I have tried to answer in the years since my friend's death. Who or what did the evil redneck represent? Who was the innocent black man? What did it mean that this person was forced off the bus? As I thought about these questions, answers finally came down to me, as if from a cloud: The racist symbolized the forces of oppression in Larry's life, and the victim here symbolized his own original innocence. The whole scene again is a memory of childhood, an articulation of the experience of an early traumatic situation in which he was relentlessly attacked and no one stood up for him. I see from this that Larry's father never opposed his mother's madness and that his childhood family circumstances devastated him. The ejection of the innocent man from the bus could symbolize the dissociation that set in, banishing the injured child from my friend's journey of emotional development.

It appears that the impact of Larry's traumatic history was just to make him feel terrible about himself. He never expressed any understanding of the challenges he had faced. That is the classic legacy of being treated like a piece of garbage by one's so-called caregivers: One begins to believe one is nothing but a piece of garbage.

There were some strange developments near the end of Larry's life relating to this, again communicated to me by his girlfriend. She told me that one week before he shot himself, another friend of hers had seen him sprinting down the road, chasing a garbage truck. When that friend had later asked him why he had been doing that, he replied that he had heard voices emanating from the truck: "Jump in, jump in, jump in!"

The relationship to the girlfriend was itself deeply troubled. There were sexual problems between them that Larry was reluctant to discuss, and he felt he was destructive to her and had increasingly been withdrawing. The girlfriend later told me that she was very masochistic in her sexuality, and could only respond physically when she was being degraded and humiliated. I had the sense that the pattern of their sexual relationship was sadomasochistic. In view of the likelihood of vast early trauma at the hands of a sadistically intrusive mother, he would have needed to turn the tables on his later sexual partners and play a role of extreme dominance and control. This would fit closely with a masochistic woman, but real sexual closeness would not have been possible for either one of them. Such interlocking themes are rooted in unprocessed early trauma for both, and this precludes real intimacy. This is a story of unrelenting sadness.

I struggle with the question whether anyone or anything could have saved my friend. Larry did try some vaguely psychoanalytic therapy in his last years, but he never felt that it reached him. In our final conversation, which took place several months before he ended his life, he told me he was thinking of undergoing primal scream therapy. This is a form of treatment created by Arthur Janov (1970/1977), a man I unfortunately came to know briefly many years ago. He was unbearably narcissistic, and I could hardly tolerate being in the same room with him for more than a few minutes. It is interesting, though, to imagine what my friend saw in Janov's approach to the salvation of humanity. I picture him crying out from the depths of his pain, in the presence of a scream therapist who could help him integrate what he was expressing. This is a curative fantasy designed to undo the dissociated trauma of his childhood: the situation of being attacked by the madness of his mother and no one being around to witness his pain or help him with it. In a way it is exactly what was needed, but Janov's manner of going about such a process was shockingly concrete and impractical. Larry needed someone to understand what had happened to him, and to understand as well all the complicated consequences of how he tried to shield himself from his own original suffering. These consequences obviously included his depression, his troubled sexual life, and also his procrastination problems on his Ph.D. dissertation. In the presence of such understanding, if he could begin to really feel it, the dissociation would have crumbled and there would have been a release of enormous pain. I see this happening, though not in an explosive session or two, as in Janov's primal scream therapy, but rather unfolding over the course of many years. It would have taken an enormous commitment of time and energy, but might also have saved his life.

Larry pulled the trigger on himself more than a year after I had moved away to a distant state in order to pursue an academic career. I did not know, or let myself know, about the trouble he was in until he was dead. In the aftermath, I came to feel I should have seen what was about to happen. I should have taken a plane to the city where he lived and beaten his door down in order to stop the suicide and help him address the catastrophe of his life and his childhood. I could not resist blaming myself for his death, even as I also have recognized that such self-blame is a kind of protection against the shock and sadness, and the utter senselessness, of losing someone I loved. Life is so hard sometimes.

THE MOTHERS OF THE DISAPPEARED

I have known a number of people over the years whose bodies were covered with scars. They had them up and down both legs, both arms, all over their chests, on their abdomens. They had made a practice of cutting themselves for a very long time, but the goal of this injurious behavior had never been one explicitly of suicide. The cuts were relatively superficial, many of them actually quite delicate.

Why do people do this? Diagnostically, those who cut themselves are often classified as suffering from what is called "borderline personality disorder," and they are notorious for being difficult patients to have in one's psychotherapy practice. I do not care for such labels, which all too often contribute to a destructive objectification of our patients and interfere with our capacity for empathy. The problem here is that when one views and responds to a certain group of traumatically injured people as borderlines, one plays into their most central vulnerabilities and produces all manner of difficult reactions; these reactions, in turn, are interpreted as symptoms of the so-called borderline illness (Stolorow et al., 1987).

I wish to offer some thoughts based on a case I encountered as a consultant in a psychiatric hospital a long time ago. The patient, a 37-year-old woman, was covered with scars from years of cutting. Her psychoanalyst, who was also a psychiatrist, had worked with her for a long time but to no avail. The patient was still cutting, and the depth of the cuts seemed to be increasing over time. The analyst explained to me that she saw her patient as a "classic borderline, with extreme regressive features." I did not like this statement, but asked her nevertheless to tell me more about how she understood her patient's behavior and what she thought had happened during the period of their work together.

The analyst said her patient showed "primitive object relations," characterized centrally by a regressive wish to merge with her mother, to crawl back into the womb and recover a prenatal state of bliss. The purpose of this regression, according to the interpretation, was to escape the storms of primitive, untamed sexual and aggressive energies that periodically flooded her from within. The patient had reported to her analyst that she felt herself "filling up" with some kind of terrible "pressure," and the only way of relieving the unbearable tension was to cut. She, the analyst, wanted to believe that the continuing and deepening cuts actually represented a paradoxical progress in her work. She told me that various "layers of defenses" had been dissolved, and the core striving of her patient had now been laid bare: the wish to retreat from conflict and submerge herself in intrauterine peace and calm.

I was skeptical about this formulation, to say the least, and asked for the basis of her conviction that the patient sought reunion with her mother by a return to the womb. She answered that the cuts proved it, for they were concrete representations on the patient's skin of the vaginal opening into which she wished to pass. She longed for the entrance into her mother's body, and since she could not have it literally, she in a sense modified her own body and became that for which she so passionately wished. Each cut, according to the psychiatrist, was a little symbolic vagina. Only a few days before my consultation on this case, again according to

her doctor, the patient had produced a symptom that unequivocally confirmed the interpretations she had made. The patient cut
herself more deeply than ever before, requiring dozens of stitches
to close the wound. She had carved the word "C-U-N-T" into the
skin on the side of her neck in big capital letters. "What clearer
proof could there be?" asked the psychiatrist. Now she was forming the little vaginal slits in her skin into the very word for the
anatomical opening they represented!

I actually began to feel ill on hearing these ideas, and wondered whether this psychiatrist was even more disturbed than the
patient I was trying to help her with. The analyst had no idea there
was anything amiss in her thinking, and she spoke with shocking
self-assurance. The patient knew with great clarity that she was in
terrible trouble, even as she continued to cut. The psychiatrist had
no self-awareness. A sickness that is unaware of itself as a sickness
is much deeper than one that is aware of itself as such. (This principle revealed itself to me in reading Kierkegaard's [1848/1941b]
The Sickness unto Death.) I asked the doctor to make the patient's
records available to me so that I could form a fuller picture of
her history. I was prepared to believe she was desperately seeking peace and calm, because her life before hospitalization had
been a bloody hell of conflict, exploitation, drug addiction, and
disrupted relationships. But the idea that she was trying to crawl
back inside her mother via the cuts that covered her body seemed
to me utterly preposterous.

The patient had told her psychiatrist that she periodically "filled
up" with unbearable "pressure," and that she relieved this tension
by means of the cuts, almost like puncturing and deflating a bal-
loon. Her doctor had an astonishingly concrete understanding of
this imagery, thinking that the pressure described was a matter of
instinctual tensions arising inside the patient's psyche. My own
view of such things is that we are dealing with intolerable affect
states in which the specific emotions involved have never been
articulated clearly. Those states are definitely about something,
however, and neither the patient nor the psychiatrist had a clue

as to what this might have been. I seem to remember some such phrase as "unmetabolized drive energies."

I discovered something when I read through the patient's hospital chart. Her early history had been one of emotional neglect, primarily, but there was also significant trauma. At the age of 6, she had been the target of a series of atrocious sexual attacks by a very disturbed relative, who repeatedly raped her—orally, anally, and vaginally. The perpetrator of this savagery said he would murder her and her family if she ever told about what he had done to her. The assaults were eventually discovered by the patient's mother, who made sure the man never had access to her little girl again. But there had been a period of months when he had his way with her. There were two terrible words that the man repeatedly shouted into the child's ear as he raped her: "You *cunt!*"

How were the emotional injuries sustained by this child handled in the aftermath of the attacks? I could find no information answering this question. The indications were that the family life continued as if nothing had ever happened. Perhaps her mother said: "The bad thing is over, and we have to move on. That was then, and this is now. We need to look forward, not backward." In other words, the incident was erased from the family history as efforts were made to embrace a future that would not preoccupy itself with the sins of the past. The family in which the patient had grown up was like that: Emotionally painful incidents were always dealt with through a pattern of looking away.

Was it a coincidence that the word the patient had carved into her neck was the very one her attacker had used against her in the midst of the rapes? Was his shouting this degrading term not an attack in itself, a verbal and emotional rape of this innocent child's young mind? But the family wanted and needed to move on. I formed the idea that the patient's pattern of cutting had to do with this early trauma. The cuts, far from being symbolic entrances into the peaceful kingdom of the womb, were concrete representations in her flesh of emotional wounds to her heart, wounds that had been denied and erased by the family's manner of dealing with difficulties by always looking away. Above all, the word produced in the slashes to her neck was a cry of her spirit and a protest against the violence that had been done to her.

Why would someone desperately need to create these cuts? They might need to do this as a concretizing affirmation that something terrible had happened, in a context that threatened to obliterate the truth. To surrender altogether to the family's denial in a way obliterates the child herself, as a central part of her history disappears and the show moves on. Each cut, ineradicable, is a form of resistance against such a deletion. The cuts are like the mothers of the disappeared in the Argentina of the 1970s, marching back and forth before the presidential palace with their posters and standing up for their missing sons and daughters.

I tried to give my view of the case to the analyst, and, as I feared, she rejected my advice. I told her she needed to speak extensively to her patient about the trauma history, and its obliteration in her family. I encouraged her to help the patient see she had been crying out about what happened to her in a physical, anatomical language, and that once again no one had been understanding her. I suggested she say that each cut was a picture, drawn in her flesh, of a wound in her heart that no one had ever taken care of. I even said she could offer the patient the metaphor of the mothers of the disappeared. All of this fell on deaf ears.

The psychiatrist subscribed to the kind of psychoanalysis that does not allow for such interpretation and explanation; instead, the emphasis is deflected away from primary experiences of trauma and victimization and toward dynamics of sexuality and aggression that are internal. This relates to the disavowals, endemic to psychoanalysis since Freud, of the constitutive role of our caregivers' treatment of us in making us who we are.

I had an opportunity many years after the consultation with the psychiatrist to get an update on her patient's fate. Their therapy had long since ended, but the patient's difficulties had not. She was still cutting herself at age 50, and there had been a number of serious suicide attempts. Cases like this sometimes end in a successful suicide. The act of killing oneself can function as the ultimate symbol of an emotional murder that has taken place long before.

One can ask what might have occurred in this case had the doctor been able to make use of what I had suggested to her regarding her patient's history of trauma. I would hope her cutting would have ceased, because the wounds to her soul were finally being addressed and taken care of. People tend to do better if the person from whom they seek help shows some human understanding. I have no illusion that such a thing would have been easy or quick. Any significant psychotherapy process always takes a long time.

The idea about how the cuts concretize emotional wounds that have been erased by invalidation and denial sometimes applies to the act of self-destruction itself. Committing suicide can be a symbol of emotional murder. If someone's soul has been murdered, that person may elect to carry out the deed in physical, literal terms. The act of killing oneself thereby symbolically expresses the truth of an experience that has been denied and erased. The brutal fact of the person's death then stands before the world, ineradicably testifying to the tragedy that no one wanted to confront. Death thereby becomes enlisted as one of the mothers of the disappeared.

There are many things that people do that serve this kind of purpose. A great many of the repetitive destructive patterns into which people's lives may fall fit into this category. A variation on the theme appeared in one of my patients years ago, who was chronically suicidal but fortunately never took action to complete the deed. Like the one in the consultation who cut herself, this patient too had been sexually attacked as a child—by her own father. As she and I were working over the initial years of our relationship, I saw something that at first confused me. She tended to ruminate about death, often fantasizing various things she could do in order to end her life. She thought about jumping out of windows on the high floors of skyscrapers, of overdosing on medications or taking various poisons, of shooting or hanging herself, and even of stabbing herself in the heart with a butcher knife. Eventually the patient began to consider stopping such thoughts and trying to create a more positive attitude toward her future. At this point, panic set in. She was terrified of ceasing to be suicidal. What emerged was this: Her suicidality, encapsulated in the ruminations, was emblematic of how hurt she had been as a child. The hurt was so profound as to strip her of her will to live. To give up the ruminations seemed to her tantamount to breaking faith with the truth of her history. If she was no longer thinking of killing herself, what then would be left to indicate anything had gone wrong in her life? Embracing survival more fully and feeling better seemed to endanger the felt validity of her early victimization. This again belonged to an early family context that denied the fact of the sexual attacks that had taken place. She envisioned her own improvement as a capitulation to her mother, who refused to address her trauma and told her she had nothing to complain about. So the suicidality preserved a truth that was never to be sacrificed—it was itself one of the mothers of the disappeared.

Sometimes we see people who again and again fall into destructive, exploitive relationships, almost as if they are seeking out their abusers, searching for the perpetrators of crimes that have been committed against them long before. Clinicians are confused by such conduct, and speak of "repetition compulsion," "masochistic surrender," "needs to do over the past to find a different ending," or some such thing. An important source for these phenomena is found in what I have been talking about. If a child's early years have been entangled with perpetrators of abuse, with recurring experiences of emotional and/or literal abandonment, and if the subjective truth of the events has been denied and buried by whatever family system is present, it is not possible to take up a more positive way of living without feeling one has broken away from the truth of history and from the person one actually is. The forces of invalidation undercut the felt reality of one's history, and this invalidation is an attack on one's feeling that one is even there. Staging (and restaging) the details of one's past keeps those details concretely alive and averts an annihilating experience of their erasure. We are once again in the realm of the mothers.

Many of the confusing, even baffling things people do turn out to be expressions of a need to hold on to a truth that is otherwise threatened with obliteration. The need to affirm the truth of one's existence is often more important than life itself. This is proven by the terrible things that are done, including the act of suicide, to prevent central truths from being disappeared.

THE DEADLY SERIOUS PATIENT

For a psychotherapist who believes in his or her work, the loss of a patient to suicide is a most terrible event. For the first 25 years of my own clinical practice, I managed to escape this experience; but then, in quick succession, two of my patients ended their lives. I was at the very beginning of the work in both cases, and did not respond to the signs that were present with sufficient urgency. One feels all the feelings that will be there: loss, sadness, shock, perhaps furious anger, guilt, fear, shame, self-doubt, and enduring helplessness. Those who say otherwise are the purveyors of denial.

I have always seen it as my sacred responsibility to avert any and all such deaths, but sometimes my best intentions go beyond what I turn out to be capable of accomplishing.

I have a colleague whom I spoke to about this whole matter of responsibility. He is an existentialist, and follows a doctrine of radical freedom with his patients. He explains to people that as far as he is concerned, the decision to live or die is up to them, and they can go either way; but if they choose to live, he will make himself available for the psychotherapeutic work. He says he never gives it a thought otherwise, and if patients elect to die, he suffers not at all. It is just the choice that the person has made. He says it is a right that should never be compromised.

I consider my colleague to be seriously misguided. He has told me that six of his patients have chosen death over the 15- or 20-year course of his practice as an existential analyst. Six is a high number, and somehow this does not surprise me. I guess my colleague hears the news of his patients' deaths, and then closes up their records and goes home to read some passages from Sartre's (1943/1966) *Being and Nothingness*. Radical freedom, indeed. At the same time, I have learned that I am not immune to the occurrence of this tragedy.

Is the existentialist right, in the final analysis? The decision to die or to live does ultimately lie with each one of us, or so one can argue. My colleague, though, ignores the phenomenology of despair. In the depths of the depressions that occasion suicide, there are no meaningful choices that can be made. The person is in the experience of an impossible, unbearable situation. There is a single door through which he or she can pass: the doorway of self-destruction. A therapist telling people in this situation that they are free to do what they please is providing an invitation to step through that door. What is bypassed is the whole complicated context that has generated the unbearable situation in the first place. One has to struggle with that context before announcing philosophical doctrines of human freedom. There is no meaningful freedom under the dark sun of melancholia. What would happen to my existentialist friend if he were to be dropped into a well, 2,000 feet deep, and then asked if he would choose to live or to drown? Six dead. On the other hand, whatever one does, there might be some deaths.

In view of the vulnerability of the clinician, how can we work with people at serious risk and keep our sanity? I can only answer this question for myself: I find I can work in the shadow of this danger as long as I know I am doing everything in my power to address the crisis that is involved. If the person ends his or her life and I know that I have not done everything possible, then my suffering will be very great. Either way, though, it will always be a terrible thing to contend with.

There are no easy answers. I have another colleague, a rather naïve young man, who reports great success in preventing suicides by means of requiring his patients to sign pledges not to end their lives. Such techniques soothe the anxiety of the psychotherapist, but do nothing for the patient. Having someone sign a paper is obviously, plainly, insultingly stupid. If I were in trouble and my therapist insisted on such a thing, I would seek a different therapist; or it is also possible I would sign the paper and then throw myself off a bridge into the water anyway. Maybe my seeing the therapist would have been a matter of giving the human world one last chance to make a difference to me. The little pathetic piece of paper to be signed might be the last straw.

One does what one believes is required in each unique situation. I have had to tackle patients who try to jump out of the window in my own analytic office. I have had to take pills, guns, knives, razor blades, ropes, and other weapons of self-destruction away from people who seemed ready to use them. I once had to physically restrain someone who tried to stab her eyes out with her fingers. I have had to hospitalize suicidal patients with the help of the police on a number of occasions. Of course hospitals are no panacea; patients kill themselves in hospitals all the time. Early in my years of training, one night, I broke down the door to a patient's apartment, because I was checking on her and thought I smelled gas. It turned out to be a false alarm, and it was seriously embarrassing, because she was out at the movies with a boyfriend.

These things are all the concrete actions one is driven to take by the immediacy of a threat to someone's life. One wants to get to the bottom of the situation that is making life unbearable for the person, but if they are dead, one can't get very far with this. So one does what one has to in trying to keep the patient alive.

A SEEMING PARADOX

It is common wisdom among experienced clinicians that people in the depths of severe depression rarely kill themselves. Instead, it is in the first stages of an apparent improvement that the risk of such a death rises (Atwood, 1972). This paradoxical phenomenon has been noted since time immemorial. The explanation I heard during my student days had to do with the energy that is available to the person. When he or she is at the bottom, it was said, there is no energy for forming and carrying out plans for anything, including one's own death. But when improvement sets in, energy returns, and there is a kind of window of vulnerability in which there is still enough of the depression left to trigger a suicide.

Such an idea makes no sense at all. How much energy does the act of self-destruction really require? Precisely how many joules are needed to throw oneself out a window or lift a container of Lysol to one's lips? The seeming paradox is explained by the fact that the patient has decided, in the secret territory of a despairing soul, to bring life to an end. Once that decision has been taken, the depressive mood will lift. An answer has been found and embraced, a plan has been set in place, and now it is just a matter of time until emancipation occurs. People become positively euphoric once they decide. Of course they keep it private, because they know others will try to stop them—at least those who are not existentialists will.

When the will to die is strong, it requires enormous effort actually to refrain from ending things. Also, how could it ever be thought that the danger is going up when the cause for it seems to be abating? If one feels better, life looks more promising, and one is less likely—not more likely—to choose death. The phenomenon flows from secret decisions that have been made, from hidden intentions that are then carried into overt action. So one only sees the surface: The person is showing outward signs of feeling better, but then affixes the hose to the exhaust pipe and dies from carbon monoxide inhalation. If you speak to someone in the euphoria of imminent suicide, you can tell something is wrong by the fact that although the person's mood is good, he or she still has no future. People on the edge of taking their own lives get all rattled if you ask about tomorrow, and next week, and next month. They are also unable to explain why they feel better. The pathway to their liberation from suffering requires secrecy in order to remain accessible. If that pathway is closed off, for example by someone discovering and taking measures to avert the impending suicide, the depression rolls back in with a vengeance.

The rise in the mood state just before death is one of the signals that is often given. Others include things like returning all one's borrowed books or other items, paying one's outstanding bills, clearing up any and all previously unresolved situations so a mess will not be left behind. My friend Larry, just before he shot himself, sent back a four-person camping tent that belonged to me. He and I had used that tent in the early 1970s, when we camped in Wisconsin at Franklin Lake. That was my signal, but I did not read it correctly.

It is stunning to me how concerned for others and how strangely polite people on the threshold of ending their lives become. Here we find a genuine paradox: There is scarcely anything more destructive to other human beings than the act of killing oneself. It leaves the survivors with lasting trauma, often then becoming passed down and contributing to terrible patterns of psychopathology in succeeding generations. And yet they send back tents they have borrowed! Of course there are no general rules; sometimes there are no indications of what is going to happen, not even the apparent good mood. Despair closes in, and death is chosen.

There are some students of suicide who imagine and hope for a time when this tragedy can be essentially abolished from the world. They picture it becoming possible to reliably identify the risk factors associated with the act—cultural, social, psychological, and biological. The dream then is that preventive measures can be taken to save the lives of those at risk—scientifically grounded interventions preempting individuals' efforts to end their lives. I feel we should always do what we can to avert the act of self-destruction, but I fear this event belongs to the tragic dimension of our lives and is an inescapable aspect of the human condition. As long as there are people in this world, there will be depression and despair. And there will always also be suicides.

7

The Dark Sun of Melancholia

*I was much further out than you thought
And not waving but drowning.*

Stevie Smith

Recently I read a long letter from a psychiatrist detailing his treatment of a very depressed artist, a woman whose chronic misery influenced her photography. She was very successful in her work, which showed a genius for capturing in pictures excruciating moments of human tragedy. The doctor told her she should try antidepressant medication, because, as he put it, "Depression is a disease that is treatable, and it makes no sense to suffer unnecessarily." She was worried, though, that taking pills would somehow affect her art. The psychiatrist reassured her that she would have even more energy to bring to her photography and that there was no danger at all. So she agreed and embarked upon a course of medication to relieve her very gloomy moods. After a period of weeks, the intensity of the depression from which she suffered did indeed begin to recede. But she also noticed that she had lost interest in photographing tragedy, and that she wanted to take pictures of people in joyful scenes instead. A problem arose because the new photographs were technically of the highest quality, but no one cared about viewing or purchasing images of happiness. So her career as an artist fell apart. The patient became very upset, thinking that the medication had indeed destroyed the basis for her art. So she stopped the medication, and, after a period, her misery reappeared. Now she was able to return to her work as a photographer of tragedy, but she also had again begun to suffer, even more severely than before. Finally, after many back-and-forth moments, she resumed the antidepressant medications, accepting the fact that her passion for her art was changing irrevocably.

The psychiatrist, in his letter, raised the question as to whether this treatment should be called a success. The patient's pain had lessened, but her career as a photographer of the dark moments of human existence had been brought to an end. Suffering was substantially relieved, but at the expense of a very creative artist's lifework. The doctor did not say what his patient had done as an alternative, but I think she found some other way of supporting herself, and cried less.

Here are my reactions to this physician's letter. An artist has been silenced, perhaps destroyed. It is to the credit of the doctor who wrote about this so-called treatment that he at least questioned its result. But it is also to his discredit, because he has suppressed an artist, whose work, like that of all artists, had a truth to tell. The patient is perhaps smiling more, but my question about all that is: So what? Who said a person should smile more and cry less? Who determined that less suffering is to be recommended over more suffering? I do not believe God informed us of that principle of life. What if there is good reason for that suffering? What if there is a context in the photographer's world that is the source of her sense of the tragic, her resonance with human despair? What if her pictures of the dark moments of life carried central truths of her personal history? We will never know, because her doctor in his wisdom "treated" her depression. I would not call this a success. I would not call it a treatment. I would call it an injury of undetermined scope and magnitude.

I become depressed frequently, and as far as I am concerned, in this world, much of the time anyway, depression is the only mood that makes sense. Here is my definitive theory of depression: It is caused by the depressing things that happen to us. Among a great many other things, it depresses me that depression itself has been turned by psychiatry and psychology into a disease process, something the medical community tells us is "treatable." Depression will never be treatable, and the reason is that it is built into the human condition itself. Human life has very depressing things within it, and to encounter these things is to be depressed by them. The idea that one can or should "treat" depression makes little sense. Sometimes I have the depressing thought that nonsense rules the world.

What about people who become so depressed they cannot function, they wish themselves dead, or they cannot even rise from their beds? Am I suggesting there is no treatment for them? I am not saying there is no help for a person in the grip of something that causes depression. There is help: namely, the support and understanding that person may be lucky enough to receive from others who care about whatever it is that has happened.

The topic of giving aid to people in depression is immensely complicated. It is never a matter of medical treatment, but always one of finding the human response that might make a difference to someone. Some situations precipitating depression are so terrible that it is difficult to imagine any response that could be of assistance. For example, one's child's suicide is an event that almost always leads to a deep and lasting depression. The idea of "treating" the resulting unhappiness is an insult to one's intelligence. If one's son or daughter commits suicide, one should be depressed—terribly, terribly depressed.

I read about a case recently of a woman whose son killed himself, and who became so distraught in the aftermath of the death that, among other things, she sought psychiatric help. The doctor prescribed antidepressants for her depression, thinking that anything he could offer to relieve her suffering would be for the best. As a result of taking the drug, her pain did abate somewhat. She felt all her feelings less intensely at this point. So-called antidepressants ought to be renamed: They are anti-intense-feelings drugs, not specific to depressive affect. But giving antidepressants to a person whose boy has killed himself makes little sense. There is no treatment for such a person.

If someone whose child had committed suicide came to me, would I tell him or her there is no help to be found? I would not say such a thing to anyone. But nothing in such a case would be within my power, because the only thing conceivable that would help the person feel better would be the undoing of the child's suicide, the reversal of reality itself. Inasmuch as I am not God, I would be afraid that I could offer little or nothing to such a person.

Perhaps I am not being fair to every situation that might arise. Before saying to someone there is no help, I would inquire as to the circumstances of the death. If the boy ended his life because he had just received a diagnosis of incurable cancer, that might be different. In the case I encountered recently, that was not the story. What happened is that the son, at the time 35 years old, had been chronically addicted to a variety of drugs and alcohol. He had never been able to make a career for himself, and had survived because his mother gave him money for food and rent. He had tried a variety of rehabilitation programs, Alcoholics Anonymous, and even psychotherapy, but to no avail. He kept falling back into the addictive patterns and relying on his mother's money. She had a lot of it, being married to the boy's stepfather, a multimillionaire. After a number of years of his continuing addiction, and of his mother's ever-present financial support, the stepfather decided that he and his wife, the boy's mother, were "enabling" the addiction and the resulting self-destruction of the young man. So he prevailed upon his wife to adopt a policy of "tough love." The boy was told that at a date certain, two months hence, the dispensations from his mother would irrevocably cease. The boy responded by thanking his mother for all the help she had been able to provide over the years, and then overdosed with heroin and died. The death was a direct reaction to the cutoff of the support. The mother and her husband tried to tell each other that they had done all that was possible, and that the boy had elected to destroy himself. It was for the best, they said, and at least now they could know their son was at peace. But as the weeks and months passed, a feeling of emptiness and despair began to envelop the mother, finally becoming so painful that she sought a psychiatric consultation. Her doctor gave her drugs immediately to ameliorate her suffering, and in consequence her pain did diminish fairly quickly. But she was now in a more-or-less numbed state, which is what antidepressant medications accomplish. Should one consider the chemical numbing of this mother's agony a meaningful treatment of her depression? As I was saying, depression is not treatable, and that is because it is a reaction to the depressing things that happen.

If this mother had come to me, I would not have turned her away. I would have listened to her story, and asked her how she was understanding her son's death. I would have wanted to know about the sources of his original addiction. Addictions do not arise out of nothing; they appear when someone becomes dependent on a substance or activity that is an antidote to painful affect states of one kind or another. I might have asked this mother what those states were and what caused them. I would have inquired about why she let herself be persuaded by her husband to cut off her son's financial support. I would have been curious to learn how she felt toward her husband now that his firm advice had turned out to have fatal results. I would have wanted to know if she felt she was responsible for her son's death. I would not have promised her that she would feel better as a result of anything I could provide, but I would make myself available if she decided she wanted to try to make some new sense of the tragedy that had befallen her family. I would know that any effort to do that might well intensify her pain, rather than relieve it.

I don't know what happened to this particular woman, but my experience has been that parents in such a situation most often do very poorly, and that is because a catastrophe of unimaginable scope has occurred. Maybe she came down with cancer and died. Or perhaps she just wasted away, destroying her body with an alcohol addiction of her own. Maybe she tried to start a movement against the dangers of drug addiction and burned herself out doing so. The guilt of the survivor that a parent experiences in this situation is beyond description, and its consequences are never pretty. I would not want to say that a parent could not find a pathway for a creative response to a child's suicide—people always turn out to be capable of something we cannot anticipate. But most often the only thing that comes in the wake of such an event is devastation for all concerned.

In saying there is no treatment for depression, I am not saying there is no help that can be made available. If a person is depressed, he or she may jump off the George Washington Bridge in New York City. If I position myself beneath the railing and catch the jumper, I have helped that person survive, at least for a little while. But that is not a treatment for the depression, which is occurring because everything has become shrouded in darkness. There is no treatment for depression, because depression is not a disease.

What about people who become terribly depressed—lethargy, sleep disturbance, loss of appetite, falling self-esteem, suicidality—but who have had nothing happen to them that has been depressing? In years past, this was called "endogenous depression." It is my view that so-called endogenous depression is a myth, a psychiatric fantasy—not a reality. Every depression is caused by something depressing that has happened, with no exceptions. Sometimes, though, people don't know what it is, or don't want to know. It is a paradox that human beings will plummet into deadly moods and all the while be avoiding or unable to look at what it is that has brought them there. Naïve observers examine someone's life and see none of the standard precipitants in the advent of depression—loss, disappointment, failure—and then draw the unwarranted conclusion that it has arisen "from within," endogenously, by which they usually mean from within the neurochemical environment of the person's brain. Strangely enough, the patient will often cling to such an explanation, because the depression was actually experienced as "coming from nowhere," as having no connection to the person's present or past circumstances. What that means, however, is that the depression has been somehow stripped of its context—of depressing things happening. The process of decontextualization is usually associated with a theme of attributing one's depressive affects to a deficiency or defect somehow existing within one's own self. The first step in helping such a person will be to counteract this pattern of self-blame and restore the gloom that has enveloped him or her to its formative setting, its original human context. There will be a painful story there, perhaps never before told, and one has to discover that story. Chemically numbing someone's mood states would be the opposite of what would make sense in most instances.

I do not want to go on record as being against the use of drugs in every situation. We live in a drug culture; it is human to use drugs of all different kinds, and I personally love them. But with regard to the use of medications in the so-called psychiatric treatment of the experience of depression, I haven't seen a lot to encourage me that it even works. I have witnessed, however, in unusual circumstances, occasions where antidepressants do seem to assist a person.

I have a colleague in my profession, a professor like myself, and he is subject to recurring depressive episodes. He has found that betting on the horses at racetracks lifts him out of otherwise extremely dark moods. So the excitement of the gambling operates to neutralize his depressive suffering. Recently he came to me and said, "Hey George, did you know that Prozac is a miracle drug? It works from a distance!" I asked him what he meant. He said that he had been very depressed recently, because his wife would not let him go to the horse races. If he went nevertheless, she would greet him at the door when he came home and try to hit him with a frying pan. She felt he was squandering their young children's college funds, and she was outraged by his gambling. As a result, he had nothing to help him lift his terrible moods, and his depressions grew darker and darker. But then his wife, who was herself very distressed by the state of her marriage, began to take Prozac, at the urging of her family physician. Once the drug was in her system, my colleague reported, she lightened up about his gambling and was less worried about the family's future financial obligations. When he would return from a day at the races now, she would even greet him at the door with a martini, and perhaps a kiss. In turn, his depressions began to lift. He said, "My wife takes the Prozac, and I feel better! It's a miracle, and it works from a distance. What a great drug!"

Am I making a claim that neurochemistry plays no role in a person's moods? Suffice it to say that every mood we have, every experience that occurs, positive or negative, is associated with its own distinctive neurophysiology. There are no exceptions, because everything is biological. I wish to avoid the topic, though, because any discussion of it in our current intellectual world descends into dualism, and nothing is to be gained from such thinking. Depression comes about from depressing things that occur.

I was talking to a medical person recently, and he was describing the depressions that may ensue as a result of steroids. He was telling in particular about the danger of suicidal depression and suicide itself in young people who take these drugs. According to him, the depressions are caused by the drugs, and he gave his understanding of the underlying neurochemistry. I have looked at a number of cases of such young people on so-called steroids, which constitute a vastly extensive range of compounds, and they are generally trying to improve their physical prowess and enhance their chances of fulfilling athletic dreams. The drive to do such things obviously will often be associated with a background of depressive feelings. Sometimes, it is true, they crash suddenly, and maybe even kill themselves. But the acts of suicide come from a sense that they have been defeated in their great self-improvement projects, from convictions that they are worthless failures—and not just from the drugs themselves. People want to find a material cause for the experience of depression, and if such a thing could be discovered, perhaps we could banish it from human existence altogether. That is a utopian dream that will never be realized. Depression comes from depressing things that happen, and that is the beginning, the middle, and the end of the story.

THE HUMAN GENESIS OF DEPRESSION

What is it that makes someone prone to depression, and then leads to recurring bouts of this awful experience? What has happened to people who think terrible thoughts about themselves, feel worthless, cannot make themselves function, and, no matter what happens, continue ever onward with emotional darkness? Something has occurred that has been taken as an indicator, not to be disputed, that the person is utterly without value, if not actively evil and destructive. There are many things that may leave a person in such a place. If we can find out what it has been, generally that will be a clue as to what, if anything, could perhaps be done for the person. If the depression arises along the pathway described by Freud (1917) in his famous essay "Mourning and Melancholia," something that in my experience is rare in the genesis of this subjective state, the help to be offered will occur within an exploring of the loss the person has experienced, the ambivalence that has colored the relationship to the lost one, the preservation of the lost object within the identification that sets in, and the dark side of that identification in the person having incorporated the negative attributes of the lost one. The depression in such a case is really an arrested grief reaction, and the person's journey lies in the realm of the completion of the mourning process. Of course this will also involve a long and hard look at the factors that interfered with the working through of the grief in the first place, something to which Freud gave little consideration.

The single most interesting idea in Freud's paper is contained in his little statement about "the shadow of the object falling on the ego." He wanted to see the self-recriminations in depression as an attack against a lost object that has been turned back upon oneself, so that the reactive fury in the face of abandonment by someone is deflected away from that person, and his/her disappointing, even enraging qualities become somehow transported into the "I," the ego, the experienced selfhood of the patient. He had this idea as an extension of the well-known phenomena of identification occurring in the process of mourning, where features of the lost object suddenly reappear as features of the person who is in mourning. An additional source of his thinking here is the theme of his own life, rooted in his childhood, one of blaming himself for the deprivations and abandonment shocks that occurred in his relationship to his own mother (Atwood & Stolorow, 1993, chap. 2). Actually, I don't think the self-criticism and self-condemnation of people in the grip of melancholia come primarily from the source Freud identified. I cannot say I have seen very many cases of severe depression that closely fit the schema outlined in "Mourning and Melancholia."

There is, however, something important in Freud's emphasis on identification processes in mourning. He highlighted something one sees all the time. In prolonged grief reactions, an identificatory reaction is almost always present, and an understanding of this helps to explain things that otherwise seem to come from nowhere. For example, a colleague of mine lost his beloved young wife and, as the months and years passed afterward, his depression deepened. Finally, after many years of suffering, he described a sense of having lost all his feelings, an experience of numbness and deadness. He went to a psychiatrist, who, upon hearing these symptoms described, pronounced the diagnosis: clinical depression. The doctor wanted to prescribe antidepressant medications in the face of this unfortunate turn in his condition. But my colleague checked with me just before embarking on the drug therapy, and I gently suggested the possibility that his depression, with its accompanying symptoms of numbness and deadness, might actually be an identification with his deceased wife, a projection of himself into the state of feeling nothing and being nothing that he imagined as her death-state. He was, as I was picturing it there, being with her in death, closing the gap that separated him from her. As I suggested this interpretation, he began to cry. The so-called clinical depression itself lifted a little as the sadness flowed in. It is so important to understand this sort of thing.

Another story that comes to mind is that of a young woman who suffered with a very serious depression. Like my colleague, she reported persistent feelings of numbness and a sense of everything alive within her as having come to a stop. Her story involved a tragedy, the sudden death of her 4-year-old daughter. She had been wrapped up in this child's life because of congenital heart problems, and gave of herself without limit. Her own emotional life became entangled with the child's physical survival, and when the daughter died, time froze and life stopped. The mother, 3 years later, had a very simple, elegant dream that captured her situation. In the dream, there was a rushing river with the water being very clear. She saw her daughter in the river, lying on the bottom, as the river flowed over her, with her unmoving eyes staring straight upward. A strange fluctuation then began to occur: Suddenly it was the mother, my patient, lying in the water, then it shifted back to the child, then the mother, then the child. The dream symbolized how time had ceased for her, as it had ceased for her little girl. She was identified with the child, in death, and within that experience felt a deadness, a coldness, a frozen immobility, even as the waters of time passed over her.

She needed 10 years to begin to pick up a life that she could participate in. In the interim, she became very attached to me, almost overwhelmingly so, because a deep part of her had never experienced emotional holding and understanding, and had in fact been emotionally killed when she was still a child herself. This was a complicating factor in the situation, that in protectively loving her daughter, she had found, vicariously, the possibility of her own resurrection. With the tragedy of the child's death, she herself died once again. Her need to be brought out of the emotional lifelessness of her early years eventually passed over on to the relationship between her and me, and she and I suffered terribly with this need for a very long time. It all worked out though.

As I said earlier, most very severe depressions, including especially the ones where self-hatred is so prominent, do not arise out of the sequence described by Freud. He thought that the self-recriminations and the self-attacks were secondary to a loss of the object, and ultimately represented a turning of a rage reaction back upon the self. Severe depressions do often involve a rageful attitude toward oneself, but the source of this does not lie in an experience of loss. In a certain way, Freud's formula for melancholia is an inversion of the dominant pathway toward this human experience. The loss that is involved is a loss of the self, and the depression is tied in with an effort to protect *against* the danger of loss of the object.

The story runs roughly as follows. The person who becomes subject to so-called melancholia, including self-hatred as one of its most prominent features, has been entangled with a parent whose emotional availability has been conditional on the child's compliance with an agenda as to who that child should be, how he or she should behave, and even what the child should think and feel. The identity of the boy or girl borrows its cohesion from the parent's vision rather than becoming established on an independent basis of the child's autonomy and agency. Such an event includes a jettisoning of the child's own authentic possibilities, an act of profound self-rejection and self-abandonment. In that way, what Donald Winnicott (1965) called the child's true self becomes lost in space, forgotten, driven away as an offending presence. I learned much about this sort of thing from my dear friend, Bernard Brandchaft et al., (2010). The tie to the parent is protected by the swallowing of the parental agenda. The power behind this structure of experience is an infinite threat, felt at the core of the child's being. There are only two choices: complying with the parental pressure and preserving the bond, or destroying the tie and plummeting forever into isolation and chaos.

A person cannot, however, abandon himself or herself without paying a price, and there is great suffering that appears when that payment comes due. Maybe a man, reacting to events great or small, begins to realize that his life has been surrendered long ago, that he has thrown himself into an identity that was never his own, and that his whole situation on this planet was authored by others rather than chosen by him. Perhaps this life then suddenly becomes a torturing prison camp, a trap from which no escape is possible. He knows nothing is right for him, but he has no basis for doing anything different. If he tries to alter his life conditions, ancient barriers reassert themselves, early childhood anxieties about desertion reappear, and, in any case, he has no inner basis for lasting change in his situation. Or perhaps a woman, responding to some shock that occurs, awakens to the realization that her whole life course, possibly even including marriage and family, was set up for her by the various people she credited as authorities. Maybe she has followed in her mother's footsteps in this regard, resigning herself to filling out preexisting roles and responsibilities and without letting herself consider what she might authentically desire. Such situations are paralyzing and depressing beyond description.

The problem in such instances is that the parental agenda, one in which there is no space for the child's authentic initiative, has gotten under the child's skin and has become a feature of how the child relates to himself or herself. Once this transpires, the child's identity, rather than forming out of spontaneous desire and its vicissitudes in the course of life events, is instead imported from without, drawn from a stock of externally defined, prepackaged images, perhaps those that constitute the parents' dreams for themselves, dreams that repair and undo histories of parental trauma. In this way the child's life becomes enslaved to the process of repairing injuries belonging to the personal worlds of those that lived before, and, tragically, those original injuries are thereby passed on to the next generation.

What about situations in depression where a person comes to believe he or she is actively evil, a demon, a murderer, the world's worst sinner, someone who deserves to suffer and die? So often this seems to occur in lives that, to the outside observer, don't show much in the way of dramatic crimes committed by or against the child. Can the story about lost authenticity illuminate such things? The history in these instances does usually go back to an enmeshment scenario with parental agendas, as I described. An added twist lies in the child's specific experience of his or her impact on the parents, in those moments during which autonomous strivings and genuine feelings are expressed, however sporadically and tentatively, that disrupt the parent-child system and induce catastrophic anxiety and unbearable suffering in the parent. Sometimes these feelings include reactions of pain and of furious anger. The child sees the destruction visited upon those on whom he or she depends, and the violence they experience with the emergence of their child's individuality appears as something limitless and devastating. This means that the rupture of the parent-child bond eventuates not only in the child's isolation and falling into chaos, but also what feels like the torture and murder of the parent. Sometimes family events conspire with and magnify all these feelings—a parent dies, commits suicide, grows ill, or becomes psychotic.

I knew a young girl once who described the choices presented to her by her situation: She could be *a live monster*—psychologically, spiritually alive, expressing her spontaneous initiative and feelings; or she could be *a dead princess*—her father's little sweetheart, compliantly harmonizing with his need for her sexual intimacy and adoration. When she deviated from the role he required of her, for instance by angrily complaining about his intrusions, his own emotional state would alternate between terrifying rage and even more frightening suicidal depression. When she made herself pleasing to him, surrendering herself to his gentle attentions, he stabilized and was even elated.

Along this pathway arises the notion that one is ineradicably evil. Freud saw a person's idea of being evil as an inward-turning deflection of an accusation against a faithless object that has committed the crime of abandonment. I am saying a more common origin is in the child's fear that he or she may heartlessly abandon and destroy the object and also in the loss of self that occurs in order to avert this disaster. This is what is meant in saying Freud's schema is a kind of inversion of the more common origin of severe depressive states. But whatever the specific sequence, depression always comes from the depressing things that happen. The sun that shines in this territory of the human soul is a very dark one, and it rises when bad things occur.

8

What Is a Ghost?

They go from me into their sleep
Yet you sleepers awaken in my heart, and a fleeting image
Of each fugitive one rests in my kindred soul
More alive, you live there.

Friedrich Hölderlin

What is a ghost, really? Here is my theory of ghosts. They are not literally the souls of the departed. They are not evil spirits that have come to torment us. Ghosts are virtual people, analogous to virtual particles in physics, that don't really exist in a positive and enduring sense, but that nevertheless have a form of being that is not just nonbeing. Virtual people—ghosts—are possibilities of who we are, who we have been, and who we might have become; they are possibilities that were never allowed to become actualized into realities. So there is a ghost physicist named George Atwood, who followed that science for his career, and who made his father very happy and proud. He became a cosmologist. There is a radical anarchist named Atwood as well, who gave his life to tearing down all existing societal structures. There is even a George Atwood who worked his whole life as a psychiatrist, devoted to his most disturbed patients. Every person carries many ghosts. We live with our own lost possibilities, and sometimes they can come to visit and even attack us.

It occurred to me that the human situation that is called bipolar disorder is often caused by the sudden arrival of powerful ghosts from the past that have been crushed. A person is strolling along in his or her life when a possibility of who that person might have been suddenly gathers power, and then it bursts in upon the present. The manic state is the experience of such a bursting in. There is an old idea in our field that mania is a defense against depression (Winnicott, 1958). There may be instances where someone is in flight from something really depressing, and in the intensity of that flight produces transitory euphorias, but real mania is virtually always a ghost attack.

The ghost comes from a possibility of oneself that has been crushed. First the person absolutely obliterates one of his possibilities, a way of being that might otherwise have materialized, and then, later, that way of being, energized by a part of the person's innermost core, strikes back against the crushing and blows the person's mind sky-high. The original crushing occurs in a primordial division of the individual's selfhood, in which one part, generally allied with and embodying the agenda to maintain secure connections to other people, comes down hard on the other part, which is at odds with other people and seeks its own independent destiny. The former oppresses the latter, and is initially victorious—but the latter comes back and has its revenge: It throws a charge of C-4 explosive into the cozy little world of the former, and then, we are off to the races!

Does this theory fly in the face of all the contemporary thinking one hears about the genetic and neurochemical basis of bipolar disorder? Yes it does, because the biological explanations of this phenomenon are almost entirely supposition, with little supporting science. Such ideas are manifestations of what in future years will be looked back on as a very dark age in psychiatry. The standard narrative regarding the dark ages is that they were times of superstition and ignorance, preoccupied with things like souls and ghosts. The light came, supposedly, with the arrival of natural science, but in modern psychiatry we have what presents itself as enlightened science, but is actually a kind of magical thinking. The serious scientific understanding of these matters focuses on ghosts. So there is a seeming paradox, but all that is superficial. What is called bipolar disorder is brought about by ghosts, and the ghosts involved come armed with explosives.

Why is it that so many otherwise intelligent people buy into the magical thinking, then, if this is true? What creates the reductive beliefs that the biology is the key? The answer resides in what lies beneath. There one finds the barricades against the very ghosts I am talking about, erected in the dark territories of the doctors' own souls. One needs to think about what is required of a person to endure and survive medical training in our country. This training is a locomotive that rolls over the personality. Every particle of rebellion and resistance has to be vanquished, and this is possible because it is so often a replication of an original crushing of the soul that occurred long before. So doctors are in the business of crushing and destroying ghosts, within and without, and they have a vested interest in denying their existence and fortifying that denial by pouring medications into the bodies of those the ghosts inhabit. Ghosts are everywhere, however, and in spite of the forces arrayed against them, they have great influence on the course of human events.

GHOSTS OF THE DEAD

There actually are ghosts not only of one's own lost possibilities, but also of the interrupted possibilities of those we have lost, those beloved souls who have died and not had a chance to fulfill their dreams, or ours for them. These ghosts come to us in our dark moments, and our suffering in the face of their inability to live becomes unbearable. At precisely that time, the ghost of the lost person may enter into us and become transformed into our own purpose in living, which is a way of completing the interrupted journey. Many of us are inhabited by such ghosts.

Often, though, the occupying ghost becomes such a presence as to usurp the one being occupied, in which case that person's displaced possibilities give rise to still another ghost. A dialectical process then ensues, ghost against ghost, a back-and-forth that goes on and on.

Someone who taught me a great deal about this matter was a young man suffering from a very significant depression, whose experiences were dominated by a theme of the inability to ask anything for himself and to assert his own will. There was a pronounced self-negation visible in his life: Again and again in various situations—at his college pursuing his studies, on dates with girlfriends, on visits with his younger brother and parents—he would become aware of something he wanted, but then was compelled to set it aside and give himself to pleasing whomever else was present, no matter what the cost to him. A kind of masochism seemed to be involved, in which he would deliberately make choices that sacrificed his own interests and caused him frustration and pain. A very extreme instance of such a choice occurred one day when he ran over his right foot with a power lawn mower and cut off his big toe.

As we discussed this pattern, it became apparent that its origin was to be found in the loss of a beloved older brother that had taken place when my patient was 7 years of age. As he was playing in the family's front yard, his brother, who was 2 years older, suddenly decided to try to outrun a passing car and race across the street in front of it. Tragedy occurred, as the boy was hit and killed. He was the mother's firstborn, and her favorite of her three sons—she collapsed into a black depression in the aftermath of the death.

My patient, in the ensuing days and weeks, spent long periods outside his mother's dark bedroom, standing in the hallway and listening to her softly weeping. Once, he opened the door and walked in, hoping somehow to comfort her. Terrible words then came from her mouth as she looked up from her tear-stained pillow: "*Why couldn't it have been you?*"

Immediately the boy saw himself from outside: His whole head was lit up like a jack-o-lantern, radiating light from within. What was this uncanny light? It was the light of life itself, glowing brightly within the young boy, in unbearable contrast to his brother's corpse lying in the cold darkness of the grave.

A dream then occurred, that very night: My patient, a devastated child, dreamed he was somehow in a cavern deep within the earth, standing on a bed of soft, pliable clay. An invisible force took hold of the clay and began to fashion the shape of a human body: first the head, then the shoulders and arms and chest, then the waist and abdomen and legs and feet. A golem had materialized in the underground cave. The patient and I, so many years later, understood this golem as the rematerialization of his dead brother, who thenceforth continued to live within him. The light emanating from my patient's head therefore dimmed, as he took on the burden of continuing and completing the interrupted journey of his brother's growing up.

The young man's difficulty with self-assertion pertained most profoundly to his having receded from living his own life in order to embrace the existence of the boy who had been killed. This is a pattern one often encounters in families wherein one of a number of siblings dies, especially when the loss triggers lasting depression in the surviving parent(s). The living children try to heal the wounded family, and themselves, by reincarnating the lost one within themselves. Such a transformation naturally cuts off their own unimpeded development, as a persistent duality crystallizes: a conflict between the need to repair the shattered family by returning the dead child to life, and the need to cast off such a burden and live out the child's own unique destiny.

I worked with this young man for a number of years. He spent countless hours crying, mourning not only his beloved brother, but also his own interrupted childhood. The light of his life slowly became brighter, and he was eventually able to live more for himself.

GHOSTS AND CREATIVITY

The ghosts of lost lives and lost possibilities are often deeply involved with the creative process. In fact, if there were no ghosts, probably there would be nothing created, and the world might freeze up into patterns of the same.

A ghost invades someone, crowding him or her out of the picture, and the person displaced wants to come back in. And so he paints pictures. But the pictures he paints might be images of his own absence, which, if one thinks about it for a moment, is just perfect. Vincent Van Gogh illustrates this in his 1888 painting, *Vincent's Chair with his Pipe*. As in the sad story I just told, he was inhabited by the ghost of an older brother who had died, and was even given that brother's very name; in reincarnating a dead boy, he became absent, his light dimmed and began to go out. But in the painting of a chair with no one sitting in it, that light was flickering and brightening, however dimly. Creativity can be an illumination of what previously has been shrouded in darkness.

Martín Ramírez was also an artist, and a so-called catatonic schizophrenic, confined in California psychiatric hospitals for the last decades of his life (Anderson, 2007). A recurring theme in his amazing drawings is that of a train, emerging from a dark tunnel in a complex, mysterious structure, and then headed into another one. The tunnel openings in the images appear strangely vaginal, with the exits being canals of birth while the entrances are returns to the womb. The train in each of his creations, phallic in shape, appears illuminated in sunlight, but only briefly, as it continues on a journey back into darkness (see Figure 8.1).

These are ghost trains. They carry the unrealized possibilities of his own being, symbolized in that short part of the journey outside of the tunnels. One can see from the images that this man never had much of a chance to establish his own life, that he was for the most part enveloped in nonbeing. The act of drawing, during his hospitalization, was probably the only expression there was of the purity of his own life spirit. The emergence of the train

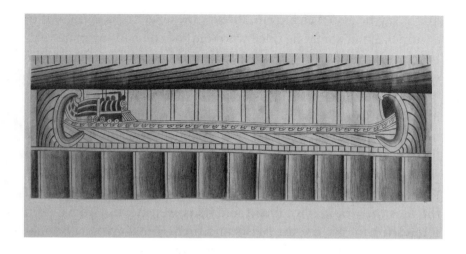

Figure 8.1 Martín Ramírez, *Untitled* (*Train*), c. 1948–1963 (18" × 47.5" crayon and pencil on paper). Copyright estate of Martín Ramírez. Used with permission.

from the tunnel is a birth symbol, a coming into being through drawing, so that the artistic work is actually creating a picture of its own function. In the long years of his incarceration, Martín Ramírez was the little engine that could exist—but only fleetingly.

Think now of the philosopher Jacques Derrida, who also had a sibling who died shortly after being born. Derrida's mother responded to the loss of her child by rushing to become pregnant, and she gave birth to Jacques. But she did not grieve, and when she looked at the new child, she saw the soul of the one who did not make it. Jacques let himself flow into the tragedy, without even knowing he was doing so, and comforted his mother by becoming the child who had been lost. But was his identity then his own? That is the question underlying Derrida's deconstructionism. Deconstructing a vision, a doctrine, an answer to any great or small question breaks open what may appear to be a definitive conclusion, a finalizing closure, and sets the stage for something creatively new to appear in this world. Derrida was always in search of the opportunity for the birth of his own soul, and his story is a sad one, because he never fully arrived. One might say he also was a train, forever in the act of coming out of a tunnel. I met someone once who told me she had intimate relations with him a few years before he died. She said it felt like he wasn't really there.

What would Derrida have said about such an interpretation had it been presented to him before he died? It would have been very difficult, because he might have felt that he had been reduced to a finalizing formula, a formula according to which his life had been precisely a resistance against such finalization. If he agreed with the idea, he would have joined in his own reduction; if he refused the idea, he would have illustrated its power. It would have been interesting to observe the twists and turns, but somehow I doubt that much that was productive would have occurred.

As a final example, let us turn to Rainer Maria Rilke, someone whose writings abound with a concern with ghosts. He was inhabited by the soul of a sister who died, like Derrida's sibling, before he was born. Consider his name, as it was given to him by his mother: Rene Karl Wilhelm Josef Maria Rilke. The name "Rainer," which normally one associates with this gentleman, does not appear in this sequence. It is a masculinization of the name "Rene," which was given to him originally as his first name. He changed it under the influence of his muse and lover, Lou Andreas Salome.

Rilke's given names form a sequence of male designations bounded at the beginning and the end by female ones: Rene and Maria. His mother lost a daughter a year before he was born, and named him and raised him to reincarnate her soul. She enclosed his name, and his soul, in a vision of a resurrected female. Dressing Rilke in girls' clothes, encouraging his playing with dolls, and systematically interpreting any and all of his early creative expressions—such as in drawing and watercolors—as essentially feminine productions, she saw to it that a child who was born a boy was raised from birth to be a girl.

The soul of the dead sister took up residence inside the young boy. Although this female spirit never became the whole of him, she did alternate in his experience with the male child he also became. Sometimes her presence was felt as a strange, mystical mask that he would put on; the problem arose when this mask began to melt into his face, becoming irremovable and displacing his own identity as a boy (Rilke, 1910/1992). Or was it the girl he was raised to be whose identity was displaced by the mask of a boy? At other times, the alien spirit erupted from within, draining away all vitality and pursuing its own independent agendas. This spirit might have been, again, the girl emerging from within the boy, or the boy erupting out of the depths of the girl his mother saw him as being. With Rilke, it is always "both/and" and never "either/or." This is an instance in which the formation of the first ghost creates the presence of a second ghost, and a dialectic ensues in which they oscillate in terms of dominance, coming together only in the intensity of creative expression. The key to the genius of Rilke's poetry lies in his ability to embrace both sides of his androgynous nature, and this ability also protected him from madness.

In the journey of the creator, there is almost always a division within the soul, one that—left unaddressed—carries the possibility of madness within its depths. The act of creation, on the other hand, by providing a pathway in which the division can be transcended and unified, is a protection against psychological destruction. There are countless examples one finds in the life histories of artists, writers, philosophers, and scientists. The need to bring together that which has been torn asunder establishes an everlasting tension, one that leads to a spiraling of creativity. This is a theme one could spend a lifetime studying.

9

The Madness and Genius of Post-Cartesian Philosophy
A Distant Mirror*

> One must...have chaos in oneself to be able to give birth to a dancing star.

Friedrich Nietzsche

If the task of a post-Cartesian psychoanalysis is understood as one of exploring the patterns of emotional experience that organize subjective life, one can recognize that this task is pursued within a framework of delimiting assumptions concerning the ontology of the person. In this chapter, we discuss these assumptions as they have emerged in the thinking of four major philosophers on whom we have drawn: Søren Kierkegaard, Friedrich Nietzsche, Ludwig Wittgenstein, and Martin Heidegger. Our purpose in what follows is to describe essential ideas of these various thinkers and to identify the formative personal contexts within which their key insights into human life took form. By psychologically contextualizing philosophical assumptions, we hope to make progress toward discerning the particularization of scope that

---

* This chapter was coauthored with Robert D. Stolorow and Donna M. Orange.

may be associated with these assumptions, and hence to begin further opening or expanding the horizons of understanding that inevitably encircle psychoanalytic inquiry.

A truly post-Cartesian theory is concerned not only with the phenomena of experience and conduct that have always been the province of psychoanalysis, but also with its own philosophical premises and their psychological foundations. The tasks of self-analysis and self-reflection, formative in psychoanalysis since its inception in the life and work of Sigmund Freud, thus acquire a new centrality in our enterprise as we make a lasting commitment to exploring the conscious and unconscious assumptions of our work. This journey of self-reflection is a matter of both the philosophy of psychoanalysis and the psychoanalysis of philosophy. We seek to raise the underlying premises of psychoanalytic inquiry into explicit awareness, and to understand as well how it is that our philosophical and theoretical assumptions embody who we are as individual persons.

In studying the psychological sources of philosophical ideas, we go against a pervasive opinion in contemporary intellectual circles that is rooted in Cartesianism. This opinion, perhaps surprising in its prevalence so long after the life and death of Descartes, arises from a continuing belief—one could almost say a mystical faith—in the autonomy of the life of the mind. The products of the mind are, in this view, to be treated as independent, self-sufficient creations—verified, falsified, or otherwise evaluated according to criteria that exist apart from the personal contexts out of which they arise. Any attempt to bring considerations of origin to bear on the understanding and development of intellectual works is seen to exemplify the unforgivable fallacy of *ad hominem* reasoning. It is therefore said that the study of the individual details of a thinker's life, although perhaps of some limited interest as simple biography, can in principle have no relevance to the broader enterprise of the development or evaluation of that thinker's work in its own terms. Intellectual constructions are claimed to have a life of their own, subsisting in the realm of public discourse, above and beyond the historical particularities of specific contributors' personal life circumstances.

Seemingly well-founded cautions about the fallacy of *ad hominem* reasoning are sometimes accompanied by a view that reinserting intellectual works into the lives of their creators inevitably diminishes those works, by "reducing" their actual or potential significance to the terms of mere individual biography. Let us regard this separation of creative constructions from their personal contexts of origin as a form of madness—a Cartesian madness—that splits asunder the unbroken, organic unity of life and thought. Let us also imagine that seeing a work in its full context, wholly embedded in the life it expresses, would add to our appreciation of that work and assist in its understanding, evaluation, and further development. The madness of isolating thought from life itself thus can be seen to diminish the works that become its victim, draining them of their lifeblood.

Whence comes the idea of this separating in the first place? What purpose can be discerned by insulating thought from being, by establishing a barrier between the thinker and the products of his or her labor? We believe this purpose is widely one of solidifying the identification of the creator completely with the creation, so that he or she then becomes able to live vicariously on a kind of ethereal plane, beyond the personal limits of his or her situation as an individual (cf. Rank, 1932). Who the creator has been prior to the work—that sad, mortal, perhaps deeply devalued or even despised human being—is overcome, transcended, and jettisoned. The identity of the creator has thus undergone a transformation and reinvention, and he or she may even imagine that the escape has been total, as the work completely supplants the life from which it grew. Such an image inevitably turns out to be illusory, however, since traces of the conditions of the creation of any idea inevitably adhere to the idea and are carried forward into each of its applications and extensions. Moreover, to the extent that the rift between work and life becomes profound, the work necessarily must become too abstract, stilted, and bloodlessly intellectual.

What finally eventuates is a sense of despair and fragmentation as the pull of all that has been disavowed begins to reassert itself. A circular movement thereby comes into being, in which the exhilarating identification with one's creations alternates with an intensifying, disturbing feeling of inner disunity.

Post-Cartesian psychoanalysis forever reminds us of our own finiteness, challenging us at every stage to understand how the structures of our personal worlds reappear in our theories. The effort to achieve a forgetfulness of individual existence through identification with one's work is thus undercut, and we are driven instead to remember, to reinvolve ourselves with our histories, to become aware of how our discoveries in the psychoanalytic study of human existence are inevitably also rediscoveries of ourselves. Psychoanalysis is the most personal of the sciences, and its nature is to include its theorists and all of their ideas within its own empirical domain. In our work as therapists, it has long been recognized that the power of the analytic experience is increased by the analyst's concurrent reflection on the involvement of his or her own personal reality in every stage of the treatment. We are saying that a parallel reflection is necessary at the level of theory construction and in laying down the philosophical foundations of our discipline.

In the history of psychoanalysis, the areas of self-analysis and self-reflection have often been sources of the most fruitful theoretical ideas. This is shown in the early stages of our field in the self-analyses conducted by Freud and Jung, lifelong explorations to which their most significant innovations were intimately tied. One could point as well to Jung's (1921/1971) theory of psychological types, which developed out of considerations regarding subjective factors coloring the early conceptual frameworks of Freud and Adler. The value of such reflection is also illustrated by the development of the intersubjective viewpoint in psychoanalysis, which emerged from studies of the personal subjectivity of various systems of personality theory (Atwood & Stolorow, 1993). Our thesis here is that the task of self-analysis must be extended to the philosophical premises underlying psychoanalytic inquiry, which like all specific theoretical ideas in the field, also necessarily embody the analyst's personal forms of being. Our approach to this great task is to study the individual worlds of selected post-Cartesian philosophers, with the aim of comprehending the psychological sources of each thinker's specific repudiation of Cartesian doctrines. We hope to use the insights gained in this study as a distant mirror to which we may turn for a clarifying glimpse of how our own departures from the Cartesian view also reflect the patterns of our specific personal worlds. It is our additional faith that such an undertaking of self-reflection carries with it the possibility of the creation of new ideas and the opening up of new pathways of inquiry for our discipline.

SØREN KIERKEGAARD

In the writings of Kierkegaard, one finds a number of interrelated areas of thought that contribute to the philosophical foundations of a post-Cartesian psychoanalysis. These areas include his ideas about individual existence, his notions of subjectivity and subjective truth, and his studies of self-estrangement in *The Sickness unto Death* (1848/1941b). Let us turn to his life history and bring forth the personal background of his thinking.

Kierkegaard suffered something, as a young man, that in his journals he called *the great earthquake*. His biographers have never understood what he was talking about in this metaphor. It was an earthquake in his soul, opening up a split wider than the Grand Canyon. This division destroyed his inner coherence, and his lifework, taken up as a result, was a sustained effort to heal the breach and recover wholeness.

The earthquake was caused by a succession of losses leading to unbearable grief. Every loss a human being suffers threatens the unity of the soul, because it confronts the person with a break between past and future. Who someone has been in a world that included the beloved is not the same individual that one becomes in a world from which the beloved has vanished. The agonies of mourning are the effects in our experience of negotiating the journey from the one to the other. Sometimes the transition is too difficult to complete, and a fissure appears between the "I" of the past and the "I" of the present and future. The former remains in a state of mystical union with those who have vanished, while the latter moves on. That is the story of Kierkegaard, who—over the course of his childhood years and very young adulthood— lost essentially his entire family: mother, father, and five siblings. There was one brother that survived into later years, a theologian, but he was unable to give much to Søren.

We were helped in understanding Kierkegaard by a clinical case one of us (G.A.) received that coincided, a number of decades ago, with a reading of this philosopher's major works. The story is of a man, 30 years old, who sought help because of an intrusive auditory hallucination. Again and again, this person, otherwise highly functional in his work and life, was disturbed and disoriented by the sounds of bells ringing out. He was asked if he had any idea as to what this might concern, and he said he did not.

He had come to the United States 4 years before, having lived in Canada. He was a very successful executive in a major corporation, and reported enjoying his employment and the life he had found after leaving his original home. When asked to tell about his background, and about the reasons for immigrating to America, he seemed oddly reluctant to speak about his past: "That was another life—that was then, and this is now—I prefer not to go into it."

After a number of meetings, a most terrible story came forth, one that related closely to the disturbing hallucination from which he was suffering. As a younger man he had been engaged to be married to a childhood sweetheart. On the day before the great event, he and others in the wedding party had traveled to his church for a rehearsal of the ceremony. On the way back, the automobile holding his fiancée, her parents, his brother, and his mother had been crashed into, and they were all killed as their car exploded in flames. He had been on the threshold of a joyous wedding, to be celebrated by beloved friends and family, and now the closest people in the world to him had been horrifically killed.

There was no real grief, no crying, no extended mourning of any kind; instead, the man went into a state of deathlike numbness. After a period of months, still in some sort of extended shock, he felt a powerful impulse to leave his country and change his life. A business opportunity was at hand, and so he essentially cut himself off from the existence he had known and moved to a northern city in the United States. Even leaving his belongings behind, he embarked on a new life and a new career. A few years passed during which he succeeded in establishing himself professionally and socially in his new country, but then the hallucination appeared. As he spoke further about the bells that were ringing in his ears, he used the word "chiming" to characterize their sound. An image of a church came into the analyst's mind. So he asked him if the sounds he was hearing were the wedding bells of the marriage that had been planned but then tragically aborted by the car accident. He asked him further if there was a part of him that was still preparing for the ceremony, perhaps even imagining that he was waiting for his bride at the altar. A number of ensuing years were spent helping him begin to come to terms with the unbearable, incomprehensible trauma of it all. During the process, it became clear that a division had opened up within him between the part of the young man who had been so deeply involved with the people of his earlier life, and the part that had embarked on creating an altogether new existence. He had dissociated his experience of the losses, but at the expense of the unity of his soul. The hallucinations of the chiming bells were calls from that former life, trying to heal the rift and bring him back to himself.

Kierkegaard too heard the chiming bells of death. Burdened with a series of unbearable losses of his beloved family members, he finally split apart, as an "I" existing separately from his family members and carrying on among the living, while an "I" remaining connected to the dead became dissociated. But he felt the call of the lost ones, who retained an everlasting claim on his heart. There is a famous passage in his personal journals that describes this claim most beautifully. It concerns a recurring experience he had while walking alone before an expanse of the ocean.

> [This] has always been one of my favorite spots. And as I stood there one quiet evening as the sea struck up its song with a deep and calm solemnity, whilst my eye met not a single sail on the vast expanse of water and the sea set bounds to the heavens, and the heavens to the sea; whilst on the other side the busy noise of life subsided and the birds sang their evening prayer—the few that are dear to me came forth from their graves, or rather it seemed to me as though they had not died. I felt so content in their midst, I rested in their embrace, and it was as though I were out of the body, wafted with them into the ether above—and the hoarse screech of the gulls reminded me that I stood alone, and everything vanished before my eyes, and I turned back with a heavy heart to mix in the busy world, yet without forgetting such blessed moments. (1834–1842/1946b, p. 3)

Kierkegaard dissociated and broke into pieces and, in the grip of his own fragmentation, was then called back to himself and to all those who had been taken away from him. His subsequent journey involved a to-and-fro movement between death and life, with no possibility of becoming wholly engaged with either.

One of his most famous works, *Either/Or* (1843), shows by its title the split in the heart of this man. The principal division addressed there is between what he designated the "aesthetic" and the "ethical." In later works, he spoke of the closely related tension between the "religious" and the "aesthetic." These dichotomies are intellectual parallels to the division within: between the part that remained bonded to his dear ones, to the eternity into which they had passed, and the part of him that engaged with the temporal world of immediacy and tried to connect with actually living human beings. If one examines how the categories relate to each other, the shadow of the earthquake separating him from his irresolvable mourning and his family members is unmistakably present. Søren Kierkegaard stood between two realms: the present world and the afterworld, and his life and work express a strange balancing act of trying to remain connected to both. Inasmuch as he could not wholly embrace anything or anyone, however, this unfortunate gentleman could really be faithful to neither.

This is seen most clearly in the tragic story of his relationship with a young woman, Regina Olsen, whom he loved dearly but felt compelled to give up. Wholeheartedly choosing a life with his beloved would have required him to cast off the ties to eternity, so he cast off Regina instead. But an inner part of him also turned back to the world and to his fiancée, holding on to a hope that he could somehow be reunited with her. He sacrificed his love for Regina on behalf of his engagement with the infinite; but he looked to Heaven, to God Himself, to make his sacrifice unnecessary and miraculously return his sweetheart to him. This is symbolized in his strange but interesting discussion of the story of Abraham and Isaac in *Fear and Trembling* (1843/1941a), wherein the father commits to sacrifice his son but the son is spared. There was a madness in Kierkegaard's everlasting duality, and it caused him to hurt himself and his Regina immeasurably. She lost the one she loved, and his heart's desire was never returned to him.

Kierkegaard's genius, distributed throughout his writings, lies in a series of things. One could cite first his reconceptualization of the human person as an existing individual. What does the term *existence* mean within the framework of his thinking? A good place to start on this is his "Concluding Unscientific Postscript" (1846/1946a), in which his famous critique of Hegelian philosophy appears. His thesis, simply stated, is: "A logical system is possible... an existential system is not possible" (p. 196). What he was saying is that a system of postulates and associated deductions can be constructed that will display an internal consistency and coherence; but an all-embracing system of ideas about human existence cannot be so constructed. The reason is that the latter must necessarily include the thinker, who cannot transcend himself and stand outside the system of his own making. Kierkegaard viewed Hegel as attempting to achieve this impossible goal, and thought it was comical and pathetic. He also pointed out that Hegel's introduction of movement into logic in his theory of the dialectic mixes the existential with the logical, and makes no sense at all.

How does his thinking here relate to the tragedy of his life? An existential "system" would be an inclusive structure, a human creation that bootstraps the thinker into an all-enveloping set of understandings that includes even himself. Not possible, said Kierkegaard. He suffered in the presence of two systems: the family system consisting of himself in relation to the dead in eternity, and the system in finite space and time made up of his relations to the living, including Regina. Neither of these included the other, and Kierkegaard unconsciously identified the all-embracing aspirations of Hegelian philosophy with his own personal impossibilities. The ultimate dream of Hegel's finalizing synthesis of the world was a mirror of this gentleman's impossible dream of becoming a whole person.

A second emphasis in his thought that made a great difference to our world lies in his formulation that "truth is subjectivity" (1846/1946a, p. 210). The idea here is that the concept of truth has two sides to it, if we think about it sufficiently deeply. One would be empirical, the truth of external facts and situations. A given proposition or belief may be said to possess this truth if it aligns properly with the factual world. But there is a second truth lying in the individual's own mode of experiencing his or her situation. Here, a person may entertain a belief, form an image, or crystallize an attitude that, regarded in external terms, appears false, but it may be held inwardly in a way that is faithful to all that this person is. Such a belief would be subjectively true.

Kierkegaard was trying in these thoughts to find a pathway toward reconciling religion and science, above all toward fighting against the discrediting of faith by "scientifically objective" evaluations. But the significance of his thinking reaches beyond such conflicts and provides a foundation for turning toward subjectivity as a territory having its own primacy and legitimacy. We believe his ideas contributed to the philosophical currents in the 19th century that led eventually to phenomenology. By elevating the subject in these thoughts, he overthrew the hegemony of the object and established a sort of balance between the two. Here again, we see an intellectual expression dramatically paralleling and symbolizing his need to integrate and reconcile his inward attachments to all those dead who remained emotionally real to him as well as his outward engagement with factually living human beings.

The third point of Kierkegaard's we would mention is found in his work *The Sickness unto Death* (1848/1941b). This is a book about human despair, understood as centrally expressed by different forms of self-alienation and self-forgetfulness. He speaks to us with unprecedented eloquence of the ways we have lost touch with ourselves as existing human beings, and of how this forgetfulness has itself become unconscious. The central feature in his analysis is the relationship to God, the Creator, in whose being all individual human beings are foundationally constituted. There is a picture in his rich imagination of the human person as ontologically embedded in the Kingdom of Heaven, and of persons who have lost touch with this truth as victims of the most terrible despair that can occur in a human life. He was, if we are right in our understanding of the great earthquake, the original sufferer from this sickness unto death. Cut away from his attachments to those who had vanished, immersed then in the immediacy of living human beings, he became separated from his own deep passions and longings for reunion with loved ones stolen away by death. In Kierkegaard's actual life, the split between Heaven and Earth could not be successfully healed; in his philosophy of despair, in contrast, a vision is developed of acknowledging and relying on one's foundation in the divine while at the same time flourishing in the world of living humankind.

FRIEDRICH NIETZSCHE

Nietzsche was a man who in the last years of his life was declared, officially and medically, insane. The genius of this thinker, however, like that of all four of our philosophers, is closely associated with a deeper madness haunting his whole life history, long antedating anyone's diagnosis of his so-called mental illness. He, like Kierkegaard, was a child of loss. He was also a man divided against himself, with a life-project of seeking—but not finding—a unification of the warring trends in his nature. His biographers, for the most part, give emphasis to the role of the death of his beloved father in his early childhood, rightly pointing to his reactions to the tragedy as an important source of his later philosophical preoccupations. What precisely, though, was the impact of this early trauma, and how did it relate to his genius and his madness?

Nietzsche suffered a most terrible catastrophe at the age of 4. There is ambiguity in the historical record as to the precise cause of the father's death, but it is known to have occurred as a result of a cranial illness or injury, and was preceded by a period of agonizing head pain. The future philosopher responded to the tragedy by identifying with his lost father and by rebuilding his identity in his father's image, needing to soothe his devastated mother and family by taking the mantle of the paternal role on to himself (Arnold & Atwood, 2005). In an autobiography penned when he was 13 years old, he tells the story of a dream, dramatically representing how his young life became swept up in the project of reincarnating his dead father. He reports the dream as having occurred soon after his father's demise.

> I dreamt that I heard the same organ-sound as the one at the burial [of my father]. While I was looking for the reason for this, suddenly a grave opens and my father, dressed in his shroud, climbs out of it. He rushes into the church and after a short while he returns with a little child in his arms. The grave opens, he enters, and the cover sinks down again on the opening. Immediately the

thunderous sound of the organ stops, and I wake up. (1858/1924, p. 244)

The child taken into the grave was unquestionably the young Nietzsche himself, now held in the deadly embrace of a consuming identification that would compromise his capacity to assert and express himself for the rest of his life. This thinker's madness is rooted in the split between the incompatible agendas of living for the deceased father and living for himself.

A division had opened up between the young boy and the paternal replacement that he became; his life course accordingly acquired a dialectical pattern, dominated by a need, never lastingly fulfilled, to bring the two parts of himself together. This is mirrored everywhere in the works of Nietzsche's genius. His works were efforts to fit together two things that ultimately could not be integrated with one another—the incompatible agendas of becoming and replacing his deceased father on the one side, and of being and becoming his own self on the other. One sees an echo of this struggle in the dichotomy between the Apollonian and the Dionysian; in the curious duality of Zarathustra (Nietzsche, 1892/1966), who preaches a doctrine bidding human beings to be themselves but at the same time himself speaks as a paternal, guiding prophet; and in a somewhat more indirect fashion in his view of human knowledge as being inherently perspectival.

Nietzsche's perspectivism inheres in one of his most famous sentences, appearing in the book of aphorisms, *Beyond Good and Evil* (1886/1973): "It has gradually become clear to me what every great philosophy has hitherto been: a confession on the part of its author and a kind of involuntary and unconscious memoir" (p. 37). The insight crystallized in this statement regarding the embeddedness of philosophy in the life of the philosopher is associated with his understanding that all our thinking is perspectival. No God's-eye view of human existence is possible for anyone, and the goal of achieving the formulation of truths holding validity transcending individual lives is accordingly rendered meaningless. A specific way Nietzsche found for asserting this idea was his well-known assertion: "God is dead" (1887/1974, p. 95).

One looks out upon impressive systems of ideas, cathedrals assembled out of abstractions, and Nietzsche tells us that these magnificent edifices are inextricably linked to the living context of the philosopher's own personal existence. There are no realities lying above and beyond the immediacy of human existence, and the whole history of proposals about such a transcendent realm turn out to be nothing more than all-too-human personal perspectives. Soaring, complex thought is integrated with lived experience, and in that unifying act one sees a manifestation of Nietzsche's lasting search for wholeness. This man's sensitivity to the perspectival nature of philosophical thought was perhaps magnified in the interplay of the dual, competing perspectives by which his life was inhabited: that of the father whom he sought to replace, and that of the original child whose identity he sought to reclaim.

Consider in this connection the doctrine of the eternal return of the same. This idea can be viewed as a reification and universalization of Nietzsche's captivity to the project of making his life repeat and extend that of his father. According to his thinking, every person is destined to endlessly repeat lives that have already been lived, returning again and again, without end, to precisely the same situations. Nietzsche's notion that he was his "father once more" (a statement occurring in his late autobiography *Ecce Homo*, 1908/1967, p. 228) precisely mirrors the idea we eternally come back to lives that have already occurred.

A madness inheres in this doctrine. Nietzsche's overall philosophy dispels the sheltering illusions provided to Western civilization by Platonic and Christian metaphysics and their associated ideas: It does this by envisioning the world of human existence as essentially chaotic, without meanings other than those we ourselves impose. He tells us there is nothing permanent we can rely on in the flux of the world's endless becoming, and such a view can propel the thinker toward a depressing nihilism. There is nothing to rely on, that is, except for one thing: the eternal return of the same. Nietzsche's doctrine oddly contradicts what his philosophy otherwise is saying: It ascribes a "permanent structure" to the flux of becoming, an essential being defined by the eternal recurrences themselves. This again mirrors how the young Nietzsche contended with the family chaos in the face of his father's death by transforming himself into a paternal duplicate.

LUDWIG WITTGENSTEIN

As one looks at Ludwig Wittgenstein's life, one factor cries out for an explanation: his intense desire to be dead. If we want to understand this philosopher, let us also seek to apprehend how his various ideas relate to an everlasting suicidality. Biographical exploration discloses something very interesting relevant to this matter. He had three brothers who killed themselves as young men. It seems very likely that his own wish to die would relate closely to his brothers' acts of self-destruction, and so one can raise the question: What happened to these people to undermine what ordinarily is the strongest motive a human being feels, the will to live?

The boys grew up in a family ruled over by their father, a wealthy Austrian steel magnate who expected all his sons to follow his own pathway and become engineers (Monk, 1990). This was a situation of overpowering narcissism in which the boys were slated for lives extending and enhancing the personal journey of the father. He was the sun and they were the planets: The significance of their individual efforts to establish themselves lay in how they reflected his radiance. Three of these children finally declined the destinies that had been designed for them, definitively rejecting a life of compliance by rejecting life itself. Ludwig initially conformed to the paternal agenda and became an engineer, and he would almost certainly have ended up the same way as his brothers had he not found philosophy.

Attracted at first to mathematical logic, Wittgenstein sought out the renowned logician, Gottlob Frege, who advised him to go to Cambridge to study with Bertrand Russell. Russell had just published, with Alfred North Whitehead, *Principia Mathematica* (1927). This new mentor figure operated as a surrogate father almost from the beginning. He was enormously impressed by Wittgenstein's philosophical depth and passion, and believed the next important steps in Western philosophy might well emerge from his protégé's work. At the same time, Russell saw Wittgenstein's deep emotional distress and worried that he might well end up killing himself instead.

On a personal level, Wittgenstein's philosophical efforts reflect a struggle to disentangle his identity from the confusing, mystifying language of his original family. He had been brainwashed, so to speak, under the usurping pressure of his father's self-centered universe. Hermann Wittgenstein was an epistemological tyrant, defining reality for all those who sought to be connected to him. This philosopher's thinking, therefore, can be viewed as a self-deprogramming enterprise, ultimately directed toward the possibility of liberating himself from the paternal agenda and claiming his own place in this world.

Wittgenstein's first book, the only one published during his lifetime, *Tractatus Logico-Philosophicus* (1922/1974), is an effort to clarify the relationship between the words of our language and what he called the "states of affairs" appearing in the world we perceive. Two specific assertions appear in this book, ones we believe are charged with personal significance: "There is no such thing as the subject.... The subject does not belong to the world" (1922, p. 69). On a philosophical level, this reminds us that we ought not to objectify the first-person singular: The "I" is not an item in the world. We are being told that the experiencing subject—what each of us sees as our own "I"—is not a content of the world we perceive; it is instead what he spoke of as a "limit" of this world, a standpoint from which we define what we call "world" and all its contents.

If we lift the statements out of their ordinary philosophical context and think about the personal, life-historical meaning they might contain, an epistemological rebellion on Wittgenstein's part appears—one mounted against the powerful father who tried to be the all-defining director of his son's existence. The son is saying:

> 'I' am not a thing belonging to your world, not anything anyone can define or control. My being lies outside the insanity of your self-absorption. Above all, know this: 'I' am not an item in the inventory of your possessions, to be made use of as you please!

The pull of the father's usurping authority, though, must have continued to be very strong, presenting an ever-present danger of falling back under his control and becoming once again the obedient extension of an irresistible will. This is not just a matter of a child fighting back against a parent who is strict and controlling. Wittgenstein's separating himself from his father was a matter of rescuing his very being as someone independently real. A crisis occurred in his young life in which he saw that continuing to walk on the road laid out for him by his father would be to become permanently itemized on the list of his father's many possessions. It would be to embrace annihilation.

A sign of the felt danger of returning to the obliterating conformity of his youth appears in a feature of Wittgenstein's life that his biographers have noted but not fully understood. It was his incapacity to dissimulate, to lie, to conceal the truth because of the claim of whatever circumstance he was in. If he did move toward some concealment, which happened exceedingly rarely, he was thrown into a crisis of wanting to immediately kill himself. Our understanding of this inability to lie is that presenting anything other than what he felt and knew to be true posed the danger of a reengulfment by the falseness of an identity based on the need to be accepted rather than on his own spontaneous intentionality and authenticity. If the only possibility was that of a false life, then his only option would have been death.

The philosopher enforced his emancipation from enslavement by cutting off relations with his father, and he refused even to accept his very substantial inheritance after the father finally died. Wittgenstein saw taking the money as sacrificing a very precarious sense of personal existence. The heart and soul of this man's madness lies in the danger of annihilation that haunted him throughout his life. We can thus view his philosophy as a search for an answer to this ontological vulnerability.

His writings, for the most part, consist in aphoristic meditations focusing on language. He gives us trains of thought that attempt to expose various confusions into which we fall, arguing that many—perhaps all—of the classic problems of philosophy arise as secondary manifestations of these linguistic confusions. Wittgenstein engages himself, and his readers, in dialogues that consider specific examples of how we speak and think and subject them to relentless reflection and analysis. In the process of these conversations, a profound critique of the whole Cartesian tradition emerges, a dismantling of metaphysical conceptions and distinctions that otherwise enwrap our thinking and imprison us within structures of unconscious confusion. Central in this transforming inquiry are understandings of human existence in terms of "mind," seen as a "thinking thing"—an actual entity with an inside that looks out on a world from which it is essentially estranged. Such an idea, once posited, leads inexorably to a dualism: One begins to wonder how the entity "mind" strangely, mysteriously connects to another entity, "body." He makes compelling arguments that specific linguistic confusions based on the human tendency to turn nouns into substantives lie at the root of such otherwise unfounded ideas.

In Wittgenstein's universe, there are no "minds" that have interiors, no intrapsychic spaces in which ideas and feelings float about in some "queer medium," no mysteries we need to be fascinated by regarding how the mental entity and its supposed contents relate to the physical object we call the body. Long-standing traditions in metaphysics are accordingly undercut, and the terrain of philosophy is opened up to new and clarifying ways of exploring our existence. Well-known arguments against the coherence of solipsism as a philosophical position and also against the possibility of an individual "private language" definitively refute the idea that it makes any sense to think of a human life in terms of an isolated "I," or ego. Wittgenstein was a post-Cartesian philosopher par excellence.

Wittgenstein sometimes viewed his scrutinizing of our linguistic expressions and associated patterns of thought as a form of "therapy" performed upon philosophy and society. It is our view that this therapy he offered to our civilization mirrored precisely the personal effort described earlier, in which his life goal was to free himself from the entangling confusions, invalidations, and annihilations pervading the family system of his youth. In this respect, he succeeded in connecting uniquely personal issues to important currents and needs of the larger culture. His philosophical journey therefore allowed him to find a meaning for his life beyond the narrow orbit of his father's deadly narcissism and helped him avoid the tragic fate of his brothers.

Let us turn now to one of Wittgenstein's (1953) most important specific ideas, that of a so-called *language game*. It is an elusive term that he never formally defined in his various dialogues, so one has to note how he used it in various contexts and extract a meaning. Of course, one of his most well-known formulations is that "the meaning is the use," and exists nowhere else, which is a distinctively post-Cartesian view of semantics.

We think of a Wittgensteinian language game as a set of words and phrases, along with their customary usages, that form a quasi-organic system, such that when one uses one or two elements in the system one is catapulted into the whole, subject to its implicit rules—in some respects trapped within its horizons of possible discourse. The German word for this is *Sprachspiel*, and the word obviously derives from *spielen*, to play. A language game, in whatever sphere of our lives it becomes manifest, encloses us within a finite system of elements and possibilities, and subjects us to rules we knowingly or unknowingly tend to follow. Such a structure literally "plays" with our minds, shaping and directing our experiences according to preformed pathways and constraining them within preestablished boundaries. Wittgenstein wanted us to become aware of these systems in which we are all embedded, and this would be part of his therapy for our whole culture. The goal is one of ushering in a greater clarity about what we think and who and what we are, illuminating what he spoke of as our "complicated form of life."

The primal language game of this man's personal history was the communication system in his early family, which designated his existence—and those of his doomed brothers—as playthings, almost like chess pieces belonging to the father's controlling agendas and properties. A clear perception of the mystifications and usurping invalidations of his early family world would obviously be of assistance in this man's attempts to find his own way. He tried mightily in his philosophical reflections to release his discipline—and the world at large—from its "bewitchment" by language, even as he was able to free himself only very tenuously from the spell cast by his father.

MARTIN HEIDEGGER

Martin Heidegger was entranced throughout his life with one and only one question: that of the meaning of Being. The great ontological goal of his lifework was to answer this question, or, at least, to prepare the way for that answer to be found. He wanted to know what it meant for something—anything—to exist, to have Being. At the beginning of Heidegger's magnum opus, *Being and Time* (1927/1962), he defines "Dasein"—his word for the distinctively human form of being—as a being for which Being is an issue. Applying Nietzsche's remark that every philosophy is a personal confession and an unconscious memoir, the statement is a revelation of the subjective background of Heidegger's whole thinking. He was a man for whom Being was an issue, a man who was uncertain of his own existence, whose sense of his own reality was tenuous and incomplete.

Being and Time (1927/1962) is arguably one of the most important and influential philosophical works of the 20th century. A central theme of the volume is captured famously in his remarkable claim: "A bare subject without a world never 'is'" (p. 152). The first half of this work is devoted to unveiling the holistic structure of human existence, covered up by traditional metaphysical dualisms, especially Descartes' (1641/1989), transformed by history into the common sense of our culture. Descartes' metaphysics divided the finite world into two distinct basic substances—*res cogitans* and *res extensa*—thinking substances (minds) with no extension in space and extended substances (bodies and other material things) that do not think. This metaphysical dualism concretized the idea of a complete separation between mind and world, between subject and object—a radical decontextualization of both mind and world with respect to one another as they are beheld in their bare, isolated "thinghood."

Heidegger (1927/1962), by contrast, sought to illuminate the unity of our Being, split asunder in the Cartesian bifurcation. Thus, what he called the "destruction" of traditional metaphysics was a clearing away of its concealments and disguises to unveil the primordial contextual whole that it had been covering up. The unity of our Being (i.e., our intelligibility to ourselves) and its context is indicated early on in *Being and Time*, in his designation of the human being as Dasein, being-there or being-situated.

Like Kierkegaard, Nietzsche, and Wittgenstein, Heidegger was a deeply divided individual, driven in his thinking to reach for wholeness. His movement toward integration appears in his interpretation of the constitutive structure of our existing as a "Being-in-the-world" (1927/1962, p. 78). With the hyphens unifying the expression Being-in-the-world (*In-der-Welt-sein*), he indicates that, in his interpretation of Dasein, the traditional ontological gap between our Being and our world is to be definitively closed and that, in their indissoluble unity, our Being and our world always contextualize one another. When we understand ourselves unveiledly, we grasp ourselves as a rich contextual whole, Being-in-the-world, in which our Being is saturated with the world in which we dwell, and the world we inhabit is drenched in human meanings and significance.

What would lead a thinker to undertake such a quest for the lost unity of our Being? Our answer is that he was searching for reassurance against the constant threat of annihilating isolation, which, for him, was built into the quest for individualized selfhood.

Little has been written about Heidegger's early childhood and formative developmental experiences. One can infer, neverthe-less, that individualized selfhood was an emotionally powerful and problematic issue for him, as shown with particular clarity in his conflictual struggles to separate himself from, and maintain continuity with, the Catholic Church and his family's Catholic heritage (Safranski, 1994/1998). Heidegger's father was a sexton at St. Martin's Catholic Church in the small provincial town of Messkirch, where the family lived under the church's care. His boyhood life was pervaded by the customs and practices of the Catholic Church. His lower-middle-class parents did not have the means to support their children's higher education, and he was able to attend seminary only with the help of financial aid from the church. His increasingly ambivalent attachment to the church was thus complicated by his financial dependence on it, which continued over a 13-year period. In consequence of his exposure to philosophy, his thinking began to stray from the Catholic world of ideas. This straying, along with the barrier to individualization posed by the required conformity to Catholic doctrine, is vividly highlighted in a passage, drenched in sarcasm, from a letter he wrote to Englebert Krebs in 1914:

> The *motu proprio* on philosophy [most likely referring to a papal edict requiring Catholic priests and teachers to sign a loyalty oath renouncing Modernist ideas] was all we needed. Perhaps you, as an "academic," could propose a better procedure, whereby anyone

who feels like having an independent thought would have his brain taken out and replaced with an Italian salad. (quoted in Ott, 1993, p. 81)

Heidegger's growing conflict about his attachment to the Catholic Church was, in the end (but only temporarily), resolved psychosomatically. Only two weeks after entering the Society of Jesus as a novice, he was dismissed for medical reasons because he had complained of "heart trouble." When these pains recurred two years later, he discontinued his training as a priest. It seems evident that his emotional conflict about differentiating himself from the church, and thus from his family of origin, was so wrenchingly intense that his growing unhappiness with Catholicism could only be experienced somatically as a physical heartache, and that he could only seize ownership of his spiritual existence by means of a psychosomatic symptom.

There are two pieces of evidence that support the interpretation that, for this philosopher, individualized selfhood was strongly linked to the danger of annihilating aloneness. The first is his (1927/1962) account of authentic (*eigentlich*) or owned existence in *Being and Time*. In this account, authentic existing is grounded in nonevasively owned Being-toward-death. Torn from the sheltering illusions of conventional everyday interpretedness (*das Man*), one who exists authentically apprehends death not as a distant event that has not yet occurred or that happens to others (as the "idle talk" of *das Man* would have it), but as a distinctive possibility that is constitutive of his or her very existence, as his or her "ownmost" and "uttermost" possibility, as a possibility that is both certain and indefinite as to its "when" and that therefore always impends as a constant threat. Authentic existing is disclosed in the mood of anxiety, in which one feels "uncanny"—that is, no longer safely at home in an everyday world that now fails to evade Being-toward-death. Heidegger claims that death as one's ownmost possibility is "nonrelational," in that death lays claim to one as an individual, nullifying one's relations with others. One's death is unsharable:

"No one can take [another's] dying away from him.... By its very essence, death is in every case mine.... Mineness...[is] ontologically constitutive for death" (p. 284). Thus, in Heidegger's view, it is authentic Being-toward-death as our ownmost, nonrelational possibility that individualizes and singularizes us. In the philosophy of *Being and Time*, individualized selfhood and annihilating aloneness belong together.

The second sign of this tormenting linkage is biographical— a poignant episode in which Heidegger placed a just-published copy of *Being and Time* on his mother's deathbed. Shortly thereafter, she died in a state of deep turmoil and disappointment at her son's having fallen away from the Catholic Church. The leaving of the book for her was a last, futile effort to find acceptance of the distinctive path to which his life of thinking had led him and to mend the bond with her that had been severed by his self-differentiating process.

During this same period in which Heidegger was bitterly rejected by his dying mother, Hannah Arendt, his lover and sustaining muse during the writing of *Being and Time*, was also in the process of withdrawing from him and breaking off their relationship. Additionally, his magnum opus was greeted by the academic community with incomprehension. These three isolating traumas, we believe, plunged Heidegger into a crisis of personal annihilation, in which he felt his sense of selfhood slip away and his world collapse around him. It was in the context of these feelings of self-loss and world loss that he turned toward National Socialism as a way of restoring himself and his world (Stolorow, Atwood, & Orange, 2010). Heidegger's personal version of Nazism was actually a form of madness—a resurrective dream picturing Being itself trying to break upon the world as it had not done since the ancient Greeks. After the war, apparently in reaction to facing the De-Nazification Committee and being barred from university teaching, he had a mental breakdown and underwent psychiatric hospitalization and treatment, after which he largely withdrew into a life of solitary philosophical reflection, his "cabin existence." His writings became pervaded by the theme of returning—returning to being-at-home or being homely, to hearth and home, and to the holy and the gods that had disappeared. In his adoption of this imagery, and in the accompanying hypostatizing and theologizing of Being, one sees a vivid expression of his longing to recapture the ties lost in his pursuit of individualized selfhood—such as those with his mother and the Catholic family of his childhood—a restorative returning brilliantly foreshadowed decades earlier in the primordial unity of Being-in-the-world. Both in Heidegger's philosophy and in his personal experiential world, authenticity and homelessness, ownmost selfhood and radical non-relationality, were inextricably intertwined.

We have discovered a striking parallelism in the course of our psychobiographical reflections on the lives and philosophical works of Kierkegaard, Nietzsche, Wittgenstein, and Heidegger. All four of these great post-Cartesian philosophers sought in their philosophies to reunite fragments hypostatized in the Cartesian bifurcations, just as they sought in their creative work to reunify the disunities in their personal psychological worlds, which had been variously fractured by emotional trauma. Their efforts to reintegrate Cartesian splits mirrored their quests for personal wholeness, and the same can be said for us. We know from first-hand personal experience the devastation of traumatic loss (Kierkegaard, Nietzsche), the profoundly undermining impact of an epistemologically tyrannical parent (Wittgenstein), and the annihilating aloneness that can result from strivings for self-differentiation (Heidegger). Our awareness of these fracturing experiences and of their impact on our psychoanalytic thinking keeps us ever phenomenological, ever contextual, and ever perspectival, open to new possibilities of understanding yet to be discovered.

References

Anderson, B. D. (2007). *Martin Ramirez*. Seattle, WA: Marquand Books.

Angelou, M. (1969). *I know why the caged bird sings*. New York, NY: Random House.

Arnold, K., & Atwood, G. (2005). Nietzsche's madness. In W. Schultz (Ed.), *Handbook of Psychobiography* (pp. 240–264). New York, NY: Oxford Press.

Atwood, G. E. (1972). Suicidal intentions and the depressive mood. *Psychotherapy: Theory, Research and Practice, 9*, 284–285.

Atwood, G. E. (1978). On the origin of messianic salvation fantasies. *International Review of Psychoanalysis, 5*, 85–96.

Atwood, G. E., & Stolorow, R. D. (1984). *Structures of subjectivity: Explorations in psychoanalytic phenomenology*. Hillsdale, NJ: Analytic Press.

Atwood, G. E., & Stolorow, R. D. (1993). *Faces in a cloud: Intersubjectivity in personality theory*. Northvale, NJ: Jason Aronson.

Atwood, G. E., Stolorow, R. D., & Orange, D. M. (2002). Shattered worlds/psychotic states: A post-Cartesian view of the experience of personal annihilation. *Psychoanalytic Psychology, 19*, 281–306.

Atwood, G. E., Stolorow, R. D., & Orange, D. M. (2011). Madness and genius in post-Cartesian philosophy: A distant mirror. *Psychoanalytic Review, 98*(3), pp. 263–285.

Binswanger, L. (1963). *Being in the world*. New York, NY: Basic Books.

Bleuler, E. (1950). *Dementia praecox or the group of schizophrenias*. Madison, CT: International Universities Press. (Original work published in 1911)

Brandchaft, B. (1993). To free the spirit from its cell. In R. D. Stolorow, G. E. Atwood, & B. Brandchaft (Eds.), *The intersubjective perspective* (pp. 57–76). Northvale, NJ: Jason Aronson.

Brandchaft, B., Doctors, S., & Sorter, D. (2010). *Toward an emancipatory psychoanalysis*. New York, NY: Routledge.

Buber, M. (1970). *I and thou* (W. A. Kaufmann, Trans.). New York, NY: Scribner. (Original work published in 1923)

Descartes, R. (1989). *Meditations*. Buffalo, NY: Prometheus Books. (Original work published in 1641)

Des Lauriers, A. M. (1962). *The experience of reality in childhood schizophrenia*. New York, NY: International Universities Press.

Federn, P. (1953). *Ego psychology and the psychoses* (E. Weiss, Ed.). New York, NY: Basic Books.

Freud, S. (1911). Psychoanalytic notes on an autobiographical account of paranoia. In *Standard edition, Vol. 12* (pp. 9–79). London, UK: Hogarth Press.

Freud, S. (1917). Mourning and melancholia. In *Standard edition, Vol. 14* (pp. 237–258). London, UK: Hogarth Press.

Freud, S. (1924). The loss of reality in neurosis and psychosis. In *Standard edition, Vol. 19* (pp. 183–187). London, UK: Hogarth Press.

Freud, S. (2004). *The interpretation of dreams*. New York, NY: Harper Collins. (Original work published in 1900)

Fromm-Reichman, F. (1954). An intensive study of 12 cases of manic-depressive psychosis. In D. Bullard (Ed.), *Psychoanalysis and psychotherapy: Selected papers of Frieda Fromm-Reichman* (pp. 227–274). Chicago, IL: University of Chicago Press.

Greenberg, J. (1964). *I never promised you a rose garden*. Orlando, FL: Holt, Rinehart, & Winston.

Heidegger, M. (1962). *Being and time*. New York, NY: Harper and Row. (Original work published in 1927)

Janov, A. (1977). *The primal scream*. New York, NY: Abacus. (Original work published in 1970)

Jung, C. G. (1907). The psychology of dementia praecox. In G. Adler, H. Read, & R. F. C. Hull (Eds. and Trans.), *The collected works of C. G. Jung: Vol. 3, The psychogenesis of mental disease* (pp. 1–152). New York, NY: Bollingen Foundation.

Jung, C. G. (1961). *Memories, dreams, reflections*. New York, NY: Vintage.

Jung, C. G. (1971). Psychological types. In *The collected works of C. G. Jung* (Vol. 6). Princeton, NJ: Princeton University Press. (Original work published in 1921)

Kafka, F. (1998). *The trial*. New York, NY: Schocken Books. (Original work published in 1925)

Karon, B. (2008). An "incurable schizophrenic." *Pragmatic Case Studies in Psychotherapy, 4,* 41–54.

Karon, B., & VandenBos, G. (1994). *Psychotherapy of schizophrenia: The treatment of choice.* Northvale, NJ: Jason Aronson.

Kierkegaard, S. (1843). *Either/or: A fragment of life.* Princeton, NJ: Princeton University Press.

Kierkegaard, S. (1941a). *Fear and trembling.* Princeton, NJ: Princeton University Press. (Original work published in 1843)

Kierkegaard, S. (1941b). *The sickness unto death.* Princeton, NJ: Princeton University Press. (Original work published in 1848)

Kierkegaard, S. (1946a). Concluding unscientific postscript. In R. Bretall (Ed.), *A Kierkegaard anthology.* Princeton, NJ: Princeton University Press. (Original work published in 1846)

Kierkegaard, S. (1946b). The journals of Søren Kierkegaard. In R. Bretall (Ed.), *A Kierkegaard anthology.* Princeton, NJ: Princeton University Press. (Original work published in 1834–1842).

Klein, M. (1934). A contribution to the psychogenesis of manic depressive states. In *Contributions to psychoanalysis* (pp. 282–310). London, UK: Hogarth Press.

Laing, R. D. (1959). *The divided self.* London, UK: Tavistock.

McKinley, J. C., & Hathaway, S. R. (1944). A multiphasic personality schedule (Minnesota): Hysteria, hypomania, and psychopathic deviate. *Journal of Applied Psychology, 28,* 153–174.

Miller, A. (1982). *The drama of the gifted child.* New York, NY: Basic Books. (Original work published as *Prisoners of childhood* in 1979)

Monk, R. (1990). *Ludwig Wittgenstein: The duty of genius.* New York, NY: Free Press.

Nietzsche, F. (1924). Out of my life (Aus meinem leben). In E. Forster-Nietzsche (Ed.), *Der werdende Nietzsche* (pp. 3–40). Munich, Germany: Musarion-Verlag. (Original work published in 1858)

Nietzsche, F. (1966). *Thus spoke Zarathustra.* New York, NY: Penguin Books. (Original work published in 1892)

Nietzsche, F. (1967). *Ecce homo.* New York, NY: Vintage Books. (Original work published in 1908)

Nietzsche, F. (1973). *Beyond good and evil.* New York, NY: Penguin Books. (Original work published in 1886)

Nietzsche, F. (1974). The gay science. In W. Kaufman (Ed.), *The portable Nietzsche* (pp. 93–101). New York, NY: Random House. (Original work published in 1887)

Orange, D. M. (1995). *Emotional understanding: Studies in psychoanalytic epistemology.* New York, NY: Guilford.

Orange, D. M., Atwood, G. E., & Stolorow, R. D. (1997). *Working intersubjectively: Contextualism in psychoanalytic practice.* Hillsdale, NJ: Analytic Press.

Ott, H. (1993). *Martin Heidegger: A political life.* New York, NY: Basic Books.

Rank, O. (1932). *Art and artist.* New York, NY: Alfred A. Knopf.

Rilke, R. M. (1992). *The notebooks of Malte Laurids Brigge.* New York, NY: W.W. Norton. (Original work published in 1910)

Safranski, R. (1998). *Martin Heidegger: Between good and evil.* Cambridge, MA: Harvard University Press. (Original work published in 1994)

Sartre, J. P. (1966). *Being and nothingness.* New York, NY: Washington Square Press. (Original work published in 1943)

Schatzman, M. (1973). *Soul murder: Persecution in the family.* New York, NY: Random House.

Schreber, D. P. (2000). *Memoirs of my nervous illness.* New York, NY: New York Review of Books. (Original work published in 1911)

Searles, H. (1965). *Collected papers on schizophrenia and related subjects.* London, UK: Hogarth Press.

Sechehaye, M. (1951). *Autobiography of a schizophrenic girl.* New York, NY: Signet.

Semrad, E. (1980). *The heart of a therapist* (S. Rako & H. Mazer, Eds.). Northvale, NJ: Jason Aronson.

Stolorow, R. D. (2007). *Trauma and human existence.* New York, NY: Analytic Press.

Stolorow, R. D. (2011). *World, affectivity, trauma: Heidegger and post-Cartesian psychoanalysis.* New York, NY: Routledge.

Stolorow, R. D., Atwood, G. E., & Orange, D. M. (2002). *Worlds of experience: The interweaving of philosophy and psychoanalysis.* New York, NY: Basic Books.

Stolorow, R. D., Atwood, G. E., & Orange, D. M. (2010). Heidegger's Nazism and the hypostatization of being. *International Journal of Psychoanalytic Self Psychology, 5,* 429–450.

Stolorow, R. D., Brandchaft, B., & Atwood, G. E. (1987). *Psychoanalytic treatment: An intersubjective approach.* Hillsdale, NJ: Analytic Press.

Sullivan, H. S. (1953). *The interpersonal theory of psychiatry.* New York, NY: W.W. Norton.

Tausk, V. (1917). On the origin of the influencing machine in schizophrenia. *Psychoanalytic Quarterly, 2,* 519–556.

Tempone, V. J., Capehart, J., Atwood, G. E., & Golding, S. L. (1966). The overtraining reversal effect under two types of discrimination. *Psychonomic Science, 5,* 229–230.

Wehr, G. (2001). *Jung: A biography.* Boston, MA: Shambhala.

Whitehead, A. N., & Russell, B. (1927). *Principia mathematica.* Cambridge, UK: Cambridge University Press.

Winnicott, D. W. (1958). The manic defense. In *Collected papers: Through paediatrics to psychoanalysis* (pp. 129–144). New York, NY: Basic Books.

Winnicott, D. W. (1974). Fear of breakdown. *International Review of Psychoanalysis, 1,* 103–107.

Wittgenstein, L. (1953). *Philosophical investigations.* New York, NY: Macmillan.

Wittgenstein, L. (1974). *Tractatus logico-philosophicus.* London, UK: Routledge. (Original work published in 1922)

Index